Yogalife

A 9-month practical approach to Yoga for vitality and self-development

Korina Kontaxaki
(Yogacharini Anandhi)

Translation by Tasoula Charalambous,
with original drawings by Anna Cosma

'Yoga is a method for conscious development'
- Dr Swami Gitananda

Contents

Low chest breathing
Asana for low chest breathing:
Sapurna Shasha Asana – incomplete rabbit posture
Middle chest breathing
Asana for middle chest breathing:
Purna Shasha Asana – complete rabbit posture
High chest breathing
Asana for high chest breathing:
Bala Asana - baby posture
Complete breathing
Asana for complete breathing:
Vyagraha pranayama – tiger breath
Meditative breathing:
Anu Loma Viloma Kriya – polarity breath
Mental exercise 1 – Mental Cleansing
Mental exercise 2 – Pause Method
Life practice
Correct breathing in our daily lives

(First part: The ideal place
Second part: Meeting with parents)
Life Practice
Perfecting the art of solitude

Physical Exercise
Supta Vajra asana (extended thunderbolt posture)
Sethu asana (the bridge posture)
Meditative Breathing
Kaya Kriya – body and breath action
Mental Exercise
Active detachment from lovers
Life Practice
Balanced pleasure
Materialistic world and welfare
Food
Sex – how erotic are you?

Physical Exercise
Dharmica Asana – devotion posture
Meditative Breathing
Friction of the spinal cord
Mental Exercise
Inner sun
Life Practice
Burning of experiences

The illusion of separateness
Physical Exercise
Ardha Matsyendra asana – **the incomplete twisting of yogi Matsyendra**
Meditative Breathing
Kaya Kriya 2 (body and breath action part 2)

Mental Exercise
Flower at the heart
Active separation from those we love
Life Practice
Hugs

Physical Exercise
Paripurna shasha asana – extended rabbit posture
Meditative Breathing
Ujjayi pranayama – psychic breath
Mental Exercise
The Self
Ultimate self-expression
Life Practice
Creation of beauty and the Three-fold Communication

Physical Exercise
Parvat Asana, the mountain posture & *Yoga Mudra* & *Shabhani Mudra*
Meditative Breathing
Prana kriya
Mental Exercise
The eye of the cyclops (part 1)
The eye of the cyclops (part 2)
Life Practice
Intuition and logic together

Introduction

Yoga is a way of life. It is a system that weakens our animal instinct. Yoga is not simply a collection of physical exercises which take place in an air-conditioned studio. This is a mere 10 % of what yoga offers. This book aspires to illustrate how we can use yoga in our daily lives so that we can *evolve*.

The following chapters summarize the work we have done (on ourselves) through the practice of yoga at *YogaLife*, over the last nine years. My students and I undertake the same procedure from September to July, starting the same cycle from the same point that the previous cycle finished.

In September we begin with exercises that expand the lungs, then continue with cleansing exercises to minimize somato-psychic blockages. Finally, we work on the energy centres (chakras) to build up energy.

The result is both constant and certain. The more times the specific 9-month-cycle is repeated, the more permanent it becomes and the more likely it is to be freed from unwanted mental programming. It is an awareness of this that inspired me to write this book, so that my students would have a hands-on practical programme to guide them. The book is not exclusively for my own members, however, as I have retained only the simplest and most direct practices, so that people who are not part of the team can follow and benefit from them too.

Those who teach yoga are free to use these practices according to their own judgment, or to follow the order and combinations mentioned for proven results.

The practices in this book come from the **Rishiculture Ashtanga Yoga** system (Gitananda Yoga –www.icyer.com) and my teachers Yoga Maharishi Dr Swami Gitananda, Yogacharini Meenakshi Devi Bhavanani and Yogacharya Dr Ananda Balagogi Bhavanani from Pondichery in Southern India. It is there that I spent and continue to spend many months of my life, learning from my teachers. This system comprises of ancient yogic practices for cleansing and reprogramming of the body, emotions and mind. It also contains advanced spiritual practices. What attracts me to this particular system is that all the practices combine equal amounts of logic and intuition. In this way, the people who are very insecure can be grounded effectively, while those who cannot function spiritually due to lack of faith can find logical explanations to support them and allow them to progress.

Sometimes, I combine the practices of **Richiculture Ashtange Yoga** (Gitananda

Yoga) with **Satyananda Yoga**, because I find that some practices belonging to this system (for example, some practices with guided visualizations) are more suited to the western style of thinking.

There are also quite a few techniques that I have adapted from different sources or I have created from scratch, according to the needs of the group and the western lifestyle.

The theories and practices described in this book relate to the cleansing and strengthening of the human 'system' (body/mind/emotions/spirit).

Each chapter describes:
　　　　A) The theory behind each subject that we are dealing with
Followed by:
　　　　B) a physical posture
　　　　C) meditative breathing
　　　　D) a mental exercise
　　　　E) a life practice

All of the above approach the theory from different aspects of our existence. In this way, for each three-week period, we have a target and a combination of exercises for this purpose, which we work on during the sessions in class but also as we go about our daily lives.

Personally, I do not believe that the physical exercises and breathing exercises of yoga or meditation can permanently change our consciousness unless they are accompanied by the philosophy of yoga. Perhaps after some exercises or after some mental guidance that some people call 'meditation', we might feel calmer and full of energy; but this only lasts until the next "failure", where one discovers that whatever had been built with their mental practice has collapsed. We need to change our way of thinking in order to elevate our consciousness in a steady and permanent way. The following chapters give a practical way of achieving this. This book does *not* contain meditation techniques or more advanced spiritual practices. It does, however, give the essential mental and physical guidance in order to meditate effectively.

"Put ABHYASA* into your practice– Regularity, repetition and rhythm - and you can change whatever you want about your-selves!"
Meenakshi Devi Bhavanani

---

*Abhyasa (continuous effort), is a term used by Patanjali, one of the first to put into words the practice of Yoga, thousands of years ago.

How to use this book

1. Read the theory based on the 21-day-practices in each chapter carefully.
2. Follow the 3 practices that are mentioned after each theory section (physical exercise/meditative breathing/mental exercise).
3. Apply the 'Life Practice' intensively during the specific 21-day period.
4. After the three weeks (21 days) move on to the following set of practices in the next chapter.

The practices that are described in the book have a nine-month duration. After that, you should start from the beginning.

It would be ideal if the physical exercise, meditative breathing and mental exercise could take place one after the other, daily, at a specific time. Regular repetition at a specific period doubles the effectiveness of the exercise. If this is not possible, it can take place separately, whenever you have time.

Prerequisites for Yoga Practice

1. Guidance from a teacher
Undoubtedly a yoga instructor will guide you better and will help you avoid mistakes and misinterpretations. It is always better to follow someone who has followed the path before you.
If this is not possible, you can contact me at yogalife@cytanet.com.cy.

2. Abstinence from unhealthy habits (smoking, pills, alcohol)
Personally I do not believe that a person who smokes, drinks or takes hormonal medication or anti-depressants should practice yoga. The point of yoga exercise is to elevate vitality to high levels - towards the brain. If this vitality is inhibited, then it is better not to stimulate it. On the other hand, I have witnessed many people who have cut these bad habits purely because the awareness and insight gained through yoga removed the desire for these artificial ways of relaxation.

3. A healthy back

Even though the physical postures (*asanas*) described in this book are simple, a strong spinal cord is still required, or at least an awareness of the state of the body, so that the exercise or the prolonged sitting postures which require a straight back do not tire the body.

4. A Vegetarian diet

Whoever works on his own at a spiritual level, will discover very quickly that the complex foods such as meat, or whatever is derived from its byproducts, will keep our bodies in their primitive state, which does not aid our spiritual aims. This also applies to eating too much food!

5. Healthy nostrils

If one of the two nostrils is permanently closed or if it is closed most of the time, this means that one of the two hemispheres is not sufficiently stimulated. The result is an imbalance of the whole system (body/mind/emotions/spirit). Try to clean the nostrils with the *jala neti* method and if you do not have the required results then visit a doctor. If the diaphragm of the nose is crooked, then follow the advice of your doctor.

6. Complete breathing

"You cannot clean the floor with a toothbrush" (Dr Ananda Balayogi Bhavanani). In the same way, you cannot clean or recharge your body if your breathing is shallow.For faster and more effective results regarding the practices that require breathing techniques, we have to use the maximum capacity of our lungs. (For correct breathing techniques, look at your notes for weeks 1-3: increasing lung capacity).

Philosophical Prerequisites of Yoga

With traditional yoga, the student lived with the teacher for years, learning ethics and working on improving his own character before embarking on the physical and mental practices. This occurred so that the student could build a strong psycho-spiritual body which would be ready for higher vibrations. It is impossible for someone to reach higher levels of consciousness if their actions do not originate from the heart – if, in other words, the illusion of separateness has not been abolished. The feeling of unity with all and with everything is what will open his conscience and will allow him to guide people with clear actions. Below, I present a broad analysis of the philosophical preconditions of yoga which encourages the strengthening of the conscience.

1. Awareness

We often believe we are following a certain philosophy, whereas in reality, the 'ego' has found a way to cover our illusions. This keeps us at the same level for years, but again the 'ego' finds ways of convincing us that we are progressing. Thus we enter a vicious cycle of illusions from which we can never escape. Sometimes we call this ego the 'survival instinct', because it conforms with our existence. **In order to avoid these inaccuracies of the Ego, we have to constantly reveal the methods with which it disguises itself.** Once we realize that there are many "conflicting interests" within us, we have to observe ourselves relentlessly, as well as the people around us and the environment, without any criticism, without excuses and without any attachment. The guru plays a very important job here: to light our path when it is hidden by the truth. Of course it is impossible to have awareness of the mind if we do not first have complete awareness of the body and the emotions. That is followed by awareness of our thoughts and finally the perfect awareness of our very existence. Dr Swami Giatananda calls it 'the three-fold awareness': awareness of the body, emotions, thoughts and eventually the awareness of our actual existence.

2. Ethos

Ethos is the strengthening of our conscience. When someone has ethos, he will avoid acting in a way that will overload his karma – in other words he avoids taking actions that will create havoc and negativity to himself or to his environment. If we generate the least possible amount of confusion then our body will be clear and becomes more stable. A person with a clear conscience expresses himself with honesty and truth. The truth does no harm and his honesty will benefit everyone around him in an inconspicuous way. In yoga there are five ethical rules which keep us from our primal existence and keep our consciousness energised. They are called *Yamas,* and they are: *Ahimsa* - harmlessness, *Satya* - truth, *Asteya* - not going beyond other's limits, *Brahmacharya* - correct usage of our creative energy, *Aparigraha* - having only what we use.

3. Detachment

In order for our spiritual body to remain pure even during our daily lives, it is vital to have an objective stance towards what is happening around us. We have to be dynamic enough to have targets that will be enforced, but to also be passive enough to withstand the flow of life. This cannot happen if there are strong bonds, obsessions, strong desires and attachments with what is happening around us. During the meditative state, one realises that life is just a projection – a dream of our higher Self. If we identify ourselves with this dream, we are simply delaying our development. We must never forget that everything is temporary. This is proof that life is just a dream. Our desires should be converted to aims, our obsessions to good habits, and our attachments to reflections.

4. Discipline

Regularity is needed in order for us to achieve the correct frame of mind, and to fight off the bad habits and those qualities that hinder our development. Unfortunately our 'bio-computer', otherwise known as our brain, does not have the ability to delete files, to change programmes and to replace certain qualities. Our programming can only change with constant regularity. Whatever we want to replace or change, has to happen with such regularity until it becomes a habit. The habit will be repeated until it becomes an established programme (character). Eventually the established (installed) programme (character) will guide our lives.

5. Service

Service means action guided by the sense of unity. It is not enough just to avoid actions that hurt ourselves and others. It is equally important to act in a way that will be mutually beneficial. This is a point of view which is often neglected. Our spiritual practices become stronger when we act as if we are a tool of the universe, to everyone's benefit. This can be achieved with unselfish service. This service will purify in a way that meditation cannot. A brilliant tool for unselfish action is the state of **gratitude**. The state of gratitude makes each of our actions a simple form of cleansing. An action that happens without expectations is pure. This happens because the action of gratitude automatically makes us not have any form of expectation. In this way we become a 'cylinder' through which all actions and their consequences slowly pass through and are removed. As they leave, they take with them any impurities connected to the action taken. Gratitude is not something that comes easily to a person, however. It is a divine instinct and it needs to be cultivated - not as a temporary state which is provoked by something, but as a permanent approach towards life.

6. Living in the now

Most of the time our actions are based on the future or are guided according to events that happened in the past. This is a quality that only humans possess. This quality, of learning from the past and looking forward to the future, has indeed brought us to a certain level of development, but now the very same quality is holding us back. The reason it is holding us back is because we are depleting all our energy of the 'now'. **We need to reactivate the ability to act with awareness but without expectations.** We should not guide our actions mechanically according to our memories; we should act according to the situation that we have before us. We should not act thinking what we can gain by this. Life is not a business transaction. By living in the now we invest our energy on reality and not on an 'expired yesterday' or an' unknown tomorrow'. **In actual fact, neither the future nor the past exist.** So the people who live their lives according to the past or the future are simply wasting their time and energy!

7. Experience not knowledge

Yoga is 100% action. Experience is very different from knowledge. Knowledge is one-dimensional; experience has many dimensions. Experience is incredibly strong and can overturn consciousness. Aim for experience, do not limit yourself to knowledge alone. Do not trust anything if you do not experience the truth that it represents. If you follow people blindly, your judgement will be weakened and without good judgement, your development will be dependent upon others.

8. Coordination with the law of Karma

The law of Karma is the reciprocation of our actions. It has no connection with punishment or reward. The law of karma is the most drastic tool regarding the development of the soul. Coordination with the law means that we can perceive that everything that happens to us is the result of our own actions and that we should embrace it, not fight it. We have to take complete responsibility for every single thing that happens to us. The person who takes responsibility for his actions may have a choice as to how to live his life. **Karma Yoga means 'action for purification'.** Karma Yoga is not always related to volunteerism or an organized charity. It is the intolerable, responsible action of our daily lives. Karma yoga is about replacing the undesirable with an active shift, instead of criticizing, asking for forgiveness with an action instead of an apology, about showing gratitude with a deed instead of just giving thanks.

9. Meaningful relationships
The people that we choose to have in our lives are the people with whom our consciousness will be in harmony. Instead of complaining, for example, that our work environment is not ideal, let us choose instead – when we have the opportunity – to be with people who inspire us. Once we have cleared our relationships up, then **we have to get rid of all the unnecessary overwhelming forms of communication** (newspapers, television, cheap entertainment, social obligations). It sounds a lot to ask, but our personal development will stay stagnant if we fill our subconscious mind with useless information which does not really concern us at the end of the day. We live in an age where we think that being fully aware of what is happening around us is an obligation and that if we are not informed about all the catastrophes, robberies and murders that take place, we are indifferent or selfish. We believe that when we have free time, an effective way to relax is by watching countless fictitious stories on the screen, or reading cheap novels. In addition, we frequently spend our energy in places we do not really want to be, with people that we will criticise later, doing or saying things that do not really represent us as individuals! For the sake of what people will say and to 'keep up appearances' we waste our time doing things that are not only useless, but also essentially harmful to our mind and our energy. All of these things burden our minds with images, words and impressions which are not even ours. As a result, when we come to our spiritual practice, we end up 'cleaning' our rubbish instead of developing as human beings. It is similar to going on a diet. First we have to lose calories without regaining them. If we exercise in order to 'burn' the calories and then eat like we were eating before, the exercise will not help us to lose weight. That is what happens with our spiritual task: we will constantly be cleaning, instead of building energy.

10. Acceptance of an invisible world
The real Truth will only reveal itself if we can move away from what we believe is real and combine logic with our inner senses. The reality, according to how our external senses understand it and how our logic interprets it is just a small proportion of the Truth. If we relate our emotion and our senses with the Truth, we are like a blind person who touches the tusk of an elephant but thinks it is a snake. The Truth is more than just logic. It is also more than our small, limited lives. For as long as we are governed by the instinct of survival, our ego and logic will always be more powerful than the soul and our inner senses. The soul does not care if the body dies. The soul is eternal and fearless. **We cannot allow our survival instinct to govern us and still expect our souls to progress.** On the other hand, if we neglect the body, it will become weak and this will not help the development of the

soul either. This is where faith is the only solution. Our faith in something invisible, higher and more powerful than us, which will cater for what is best, and is an essential quality in our advanced stage of development. It might not be necessary from the outset, but when our souls finally have strength within us, our faith is what will give us security and courage to move on. Otherwise fear will always hold us back.

"For my cells, I am God.
Do they also wonder if I exist?"
Dr. Ananda Balayogi Bhavanani

Weeks 1-3 Hathenas
Correct breathing/increasing the capacity of the lungs
(from the Gitananda Yoga tradition)

In the first three weeks, we use a special group of postures and exercises which are called *Hathenas*. We use them in order to expand the capacity of the lungs, opening them. As a result, our system is directly cleansed, which is why some people may feel discomfort, boredom or headaches at the start, until the physical, mental and emotional toxins are cleared, and this is where the opening of the lungs can begin to increase our vitality. The cleansing of the system and the increase of vitality through the hathenas, is vital for the effective outcome of our yoga practice.

The lungs can be divided into 3 parts (low, middle and high), and we can choose whether to use these three parts separately or together when we are breathing.

Therefore, we have three types of breathing:

1. Diaphragmatic or abdominal breathing
2. Thoracic or middle chest breathing
3. Upper chest or higher chest breathing

First we learn to use ONE section of the lungs for each breath, and then we use all three parts with complete breathing.

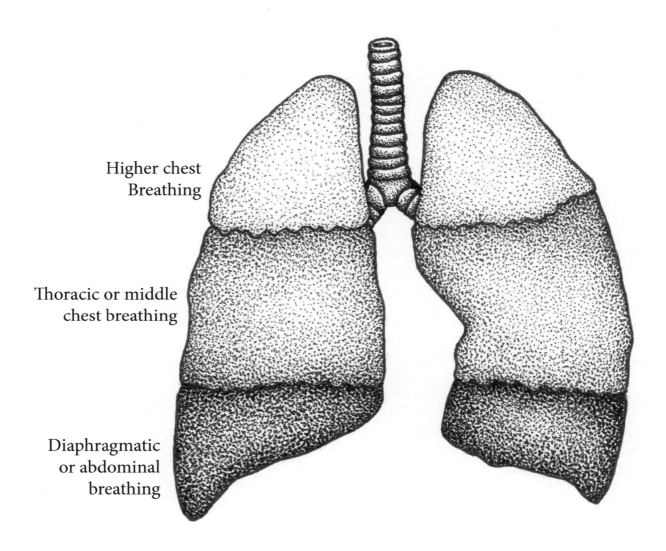

Higher chest
Breathing

Thoracic or middle
chest breathing

Diaphragmatic
or abdominal
breathing

We combine the *hathenas* – the exercises for the opening of the lungs - with breathing and mental exercises for cleansing. In this way we can speed up the cleansing process, which is key to the continuation of our practices.

Vajra Asana

This posture is called *Vajra Asana* and it is used for meditative breathing but also mental exercise. The spine must remain upright, with the pelvis aligned. The heels should be connected so that we sit on our heels, not our feet. *Vajra asana* increases blood circulation to the pelvis and stomach, cleansing and activating our sacrum and our solar plexus - areas that are vital for concentration and our energetic strength.

Diaphragmatic or Abdominal Breathing

Kneel down in the *Vajra Asana* position (p.27), or lie on your back.

Put your right hand on your abdominal area, and your left hand on your chest. Remove all the air from your lungs. Feel the lower lungs in your body - they are located behind the ribs, above the abdomen.

Now breathe in using the lower part of the lungs so that the belly expands. Your left hand, which is on your chest, should not move. Hold the breath for a second. Breathe out pressing the belly (by lifting the diaphragm*) so that the lower lungs are emptied. Before you breathe in again, keep the lungs empty for a second.

Realise your diaphragm: an elastic muscle which is located under the lungs. The diaphragm goes down when we inhale, massaging our abdominal organs (liver, stomach, bowels) as it does so and pushing these organs outwards when the belly is inflated.

Asana for abdominal breathing:
Sapurna Shasha Asana – Incomplete Rabbit Posture

This posture strengthens the lower part of the lungs. In this position, we will be able to feel our abdominal breathing more intensely. Feel where your lower lungs are situated in your body. They are behind your ribcage, just above your belly button. It is important to be able to feel the lower lungs expanding inside the body, and pushing the abdominal organs outwards. Abdominal breathing activates and energises the physical body, particularly the digestive system and the abdominal/pelvic organs.

Thoracic or Middle Chest Breathing

Kneel down in the *Vajra Asana* position (p.27). Focus on the ribcage. Contract and tighten the belly. Gently and slowly breathe in so that the chest expands. The diaphragm and the belly must not move. Hold your breath for a second. Breathe out slowly, relaxing the chest muscles. Hold your breath for a second before breathing in again.

Asana for middle chest breathing:
Purna Shasha Asana- Final Rabbit Posture

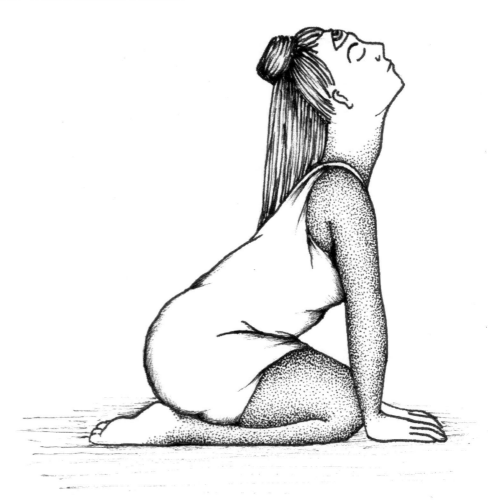

This position strengthens the middle part of the lungs. In this position you can easily feel the middle chest breathing. Try to feel where the middle lungs are located. They are behind the chest, at the level of the heart. It is very important that you feel the middle lungs expanding within your body, lifting your chest. Middle chest breathing activates and energises the emotional body (*pranayama kosha*) and the heart.

Upper or Higher Chest Breathing

Kneel down in *Vajra Asana* (p.27), or lie on your back.
Concentrate on the upper part of the lungs within your body: they are above the chest and under your armpits. Contract and tighten your belly gently. Breathe in in such a way that your shoulders rise lightly and the collar bone opens. The belly must not move, the chest rises slowly. Hold your breath for a while. Relax your shoulders and your breath so you can breathe more gently and steadily. Hold your out-breath for a while before you breathe in again.

Asana for Higher Chest Breathing:
Bala Asana – Child Pose

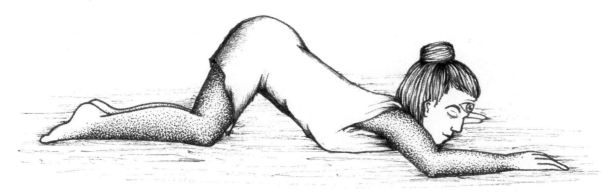

This pose strengthens the upper part of the lungs. We can easily feel the higher chest breathing. Try to feel where the upper lungs are located within the body: a little further down from the base of the neck. It is important that you can feel the upper lungs expanding in your body, moving the chest upwards. Upper chest breathing activates the body, face, neck and brain.

Complete Breathing

Sectional breathing will help strengthen the lungs and enable us to apply complete breathing.

The correct way to breath is by complete breathing, using all parts of the lungs equally in the following order:

We breathe in from: a) the abdominal b) the middle chest c) the upper chest
We breathe out from: a) the abdominal b) the middle chest c) the upper chest

Asana for Complete Breathing:

Vyagraha Pranayama – Tiger's Breath

Get down on all fours as shown in the picture. 'Open' your body slowly filling your lower, middle and upper lungs with air. Hold the position and the breath for 1-2 seconds. Then 'close' your body letting the air out slowly from the lower, middle and upper parts of the lungs. Hold the position and the breath for 1-2 seconds. Allow the movement to open and close the lungs and do not suck in or force the air in any way. Just allow the lungs to open. This will make your breath calm, conscious and silent.

Meditative Breathing
Anu Loma-Viloma Pranayama - Polarity Breath
(From the Gitananda Yoga tradition)

The human body is created to have perfect polarity. The modern human being may have lost this quality for many reasons: because of the lack of contact with nature, the consumption of processed food, too much stress that is not released, the disturbed hormonal system and our constant negative feelings which may be kept locked inside of us, often not by choice. The result of this lack of polarity is illness, depression and lack of concentration. This, of course, is very profitable for the pharmaceutical companies that have made a fortune by selling antibiotics, anti-depressants, synthetic vitamins and lots of other pills to 'cure' the above-mentioned ailments.

There is a more effective way to charge our system however: using breath combined with visualisations. If you can perfect the following exercise and include it in your daily routine, you won't even remember the last time you were sick or depressed without good reason.

This is the most basic meditative breath that we will use both as an introduction and as a basis for all the other meditative breaths that follow. This breath balances the nervous system and the cells of the body, giving "neutral polarity"; in other words, a strong but balanced charging of the body.

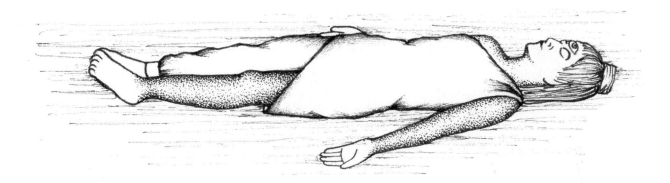

Shava Asana

Shava Asana: We lie down on our backs with our heads facing north, our heels together, our arms close to our bodies and the palms of the hands facing upward.

31

Main Meditative Breathing (*Anu Loma-Viloma Pranayama* - **Polarity Breath**)

Lie down in *Shava Asana* (p.32) or sit in a meditative position with your spine straight. Your direction is towards the north. Start with a complete rhythmic breath: Our in-breath should have the same duration as the out-breath and we should hold each one for half the time. The best rhythm is 6:3:6:3 – in other words, breathe in for 6 seconds and hold the breath for 3 seconds, breathe out for 6 seconds and hold the breath for 3 seconds. This rhythm is ideal for us to absorb the *prana* (energy) from the air and to balance our emotional body. If the pace appears too slow, start with 4:2:4:2 until you get used to it.

After a few rounds of rhythmic breaths add a mental activity:

When using *Shava Asana* (p.32):
With your in-breath, feel or visualise a red or gold warm wave of energy passing over and showering your body from your head to your feet. When the in-breath is complete, the red or gold wave should have gone beyond your feet. With your out-breath, feel or visualise a blue or silver, cool wave of energy passing over and showering your body from your feet to your head. When the out-breath is complete, the blue or silver wave should have gone beyond your head. When you hold your in-breath and out-breath, the colours and energy remain steady and move beyond the feet and beyond the head.

When using any other meditative posture:
With your in-breath, feel or visualise a red or gold warm wave of energy passing over and showering your body from your head towards your pelvis. When the in-breath is complete, the red or gold wave should have gone beyond your pelvis, to the ground. With your out-breath, feel or visualise a blue or silver, cool wave of energy passing over and showering your body from your pelvis to your head. When the out-breath is complete, the blue or silver wave should have gone beyond your head. When you hold your in-breath and out-breath, the colours and energy remain steady and move beyond the pelvis and beyond the head.

Repeat this approximately 9 times or as many times as you need till you get the feeling of static electricity over your body. This means that the system has the correct polarity.

Note: with the polarity breath you ALWAYS inhale and exhale through the nose, and always with complete breathing.

Start the exercise by doing 9 rounds of breaths for 9 continual days. Then increase this to 18 rounds for another 9 days and then to 27 rounds for a further 9 days, with the 6:3:6:3 pace. After that you will have perfected the exercise and the practice will be 'saved' in the system like a programme. Then you will only need to do 9 rounds of 6:3:6:3. The 9 rounds do not last more than 5 minutes and in this way you will have 'charged' the body for the next 4 hours!

Many people have a problem sleeping after this exercise. If this happens to you, find a way to use this time wisely, and do not worry that you are not getting enough sleep. You simply do not need it. This time will be more creative and productive. Others, on the other hand, use this exercise so they can sleep more calmly and deeply. In other words, this exercise gives us what we actually need!

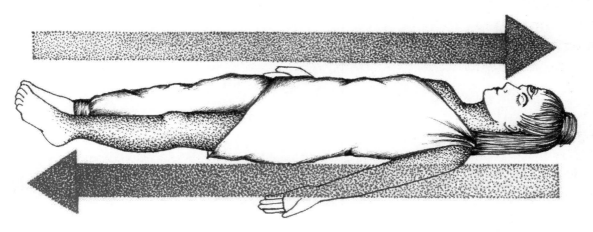

Anu Loma Viloma Pranayama

Mental Exercise 1
Mental Cleansing
(The practices mentioned below are based on the *Nadi Jnana Kriya* from the Gitananda Yoga Tradition)

Choose *one* of the following each time:

1. Imagine that you are lying alongside a river and the water is flowing over your head towards your feet and then moves on. At the beginning the water is dirty (e.g. filled with soil, stones, rubbish) but after a while the water starts to get cleaner and cleaner and finally becomes completely clear, cool and refreshing.

2. Sit with your back straight. Make sure that your spinal cord is erect. Now imagine that the spinal cord is a cylinder and that the tail bone goes into the ground. So one end of the cylinder is in the ground and the other part ends up in a cave where the brain is. Allow all feelings of tension, thoughts and images that are not necessary, to pass through this cylinder from the brain to the ground. Keep the flow going until you feel that you have cleansed them all.

Mental Exercise 2
The Pause method
(based on the *Four-Fold Awareness* from the Gitananda Yoga Tradition)

Take a break from whatever it is you are doing at least three times a day. This practice takes from 1 to 3 minutes and is very useful as it reminds us that we are not our thoughts.

Stay still for a moment. If you can, close your eyes. Focus for a few seconds on the noise around you. Do not try to classify it as good or bad, just listen. Then try to concentrate on the shape of your body. Mentally draw the outline of your body and try to feel the shape.

Now concentrate on your breath. Be aware of your breathing. Feel the lungs expanding when you inhale and shrinking when you exhale. Then concentrate on the shape of your body and finally the noise around you for a few seconds.

The 'pause' is now complete. You may continue with your day.

Life Practice
Breathing in our everyday life

Consciously become aware of your breathing during the day. Every now and again take some complete breaths. Try to 'chew' and 'digest' the air. In other words, try to keep the air within you for a while (chewing) before you eject it and keep your lungs empty for a while (digesting) before breathing in again.

Try to connect your breath with your thoughts. Allow your breathing to help your mental and emotional state. Inhale whatever you want inside you, and exhale whatever you want to unload. Every time, for example, you have a negative thought, try to remove it by exhaling it. Every time you see something beautiful, inhale it so that it can enter your body.

Feel which actions and feelings charge or burden your system. Each time you feel an overwhelming feeling, (whether positive or negative) concentrate on your breath so you can balance it (neutral polarity). You will see that after a few moments the mind clears and you can act more correctly. Numerous misunderstandings or bad decisions are made due to our enthusiasm or our rage.

The Three Major Consumers
Food, Sex, Relationships

According to the ancient theories of yoga, the human body consists of five interdependent and interconnected layers or bodies which in Sanskrit are called *Koshas*:

1. ***Annamaya Kosha*** – The physical body 'made' of food
2. ***Pranamaya Kosha*** – The emotional body 'made' of ether (vitality)
3. ***Mannomaya Kosha*** – The mental body 'made' of memory/knowledge/programming (conscious and subconscious mind)
4. ***Vijnanamaya Kosha*** – The higher mental body 'made' of wisdom (super conscious mind)
5. ***Anandamaya Kosha*** – The spiritual body 'made' of bliss

Imagine all of these five systems as one high-tech machine which is controlled by a high-tech biocomputer – our brain. Where does this machine get its energy from? What kind of energy does it need to check and to operate this system?

Most of us believe that the only way that the brain gets energy is from food, and that energy can be counted in calories. And yet, calories, and generally, carbohydrates, proteins and fats, are needed only for our physical body, which is just one-fifth of our existence!

The brain requires a type of 'human electricity' which is called prana or ether or vitality so that it can programme the functions of our five bodies. Prana is the live energy which exists in the air and in the sun mainly, but also in plants since they need air and sun to thrive. In humans, more than 60% of the absorption of Prana occurs with complete breathing and only the remaining proportion is absorbed from food and other sources. However, the average human uses a small percentage of his lungs; therefore he gets only a small proportion of energy from Prana. In addition, although digestion gives us the physical energy we need, it requires great mental energy, which of course requires Prana. The energy which theoretically is attributed to food, does not include the energy loss of the digestive and urinary system.

Pancha Koshas *– The five bodies of the human system: Physical Body, Emotional Body, Mental Body, Higher Mental Body, Spiritual Body*

Scientists say that our brain requires 20% of the body's total energy requirements so it can function. But this only applies to a brain that serves a 3-dimensonal material world that needs energy just for materialistic and basic mental activities. Our other 'bodies' (emotional, higher mental, spiritual) also need the brain as a medium and thrive on Prana/vitality. In reality, the brain needs 20% food and 80% Prana. The requirements of the brain for Prana are not satisfied so the brain 'disconnects' the functions that are not necessary for survival (but are vital for human development) so that it can use the energy for the essentials (reproduction, metabolism, movement of the body, memory, communication etc).

This kind of "cell memory" is installed in most people, even if we have our survival needs covered. **The brain, instinctively focuses on the three things essential for survival: food, sex and relationships.**

The three major consumers are three parts of our existence which, due to ancient programming, take up most of our attention, consuming our *Prana* (vitality). So to 'economise' our brain gets weaker and disconnects the 'higher' centre which is responsible for our development. These three areas of the body become overloaded with the wrong kind of attention and in the end become blocked. Compare them to very busy roundabouts. If there is no organisation or if there are no rules, the roundabouts will become jammed with cars that will not be able to move. The three areas are the stomach (food/power), the pelvis (sex, pleasure, desires) and the neck (relationships, self-expression).

The reprogramming and the release of the brain from the three great consumers occurs slowly through the practice of *Abhyasa* (regularity, repetition, rhythm) so new habits can be created. If we attempt to cut the supply of energy to any of these three "consumers", the body will react, consuming even more energy. Nine to twelve months are needed for the body to re-adjust. We work with specific practices which help clear the obstacles from these three areas (stomach/pelvis/neck) and do exercises that increase vitality (prana). The most important one is the life practice: it is necessary to understand that the material body is imposed on by the other layers of our existence (emotions, mind, soul).

The emotions, mind and soul are not just part of the material world but have their own equal dimensions. Most people believe that everything is found within the body and that the soul does not exist. They have stopped nurturing the invisible body with the mentality that if they feed the physical body, then the body will look after everything else. This is a complete misconception; it is the invisible, higher body which has the power to feed the system. We have left all the responsibility of our existence to the body and that is why we get sick and the brain cannot control the illness; we want to eat when what we actually need is love, and we are afraid when all we need to do is give *prana* to each other. It's free!

Weeks 4-6
First Major Consumer: Food
Part of the body: Stomach/ Solar Plexus

The solar plexus is located below the stomach, just a few centimetres above the belly button. It is the area that absorbs, processes and distributes **food, experiences, prana.**

Food

Dr Swami Gitananda would say, 'You can eat whatever you want, as long as you can digest it.' Do we really digest our food, or do we simply load our stomach with too much food which is only half-digested, creating toxins in the body?

The food we eat has become more of a social, psychological and mental need rather than a physical one. It actually uses up more energy than it gives. We have become so addicted to food and this is draining our energy. It is almost like we are trying to compensate for the hunger and anxiety our ancestors had when they were searching for food. This not only harms our bodies since we end up with extra kilos and various health issues, but also the soul, since no time or energy is left for it to express itself.

Impressions/Experiences

All the information from our day 'enters' our bodies through the solar plexus. In the same way that the stomach digests food, the solar plexus 'digests' information (thoughts, emotions, facts) and distributes them to our invisible bodies (mental and emotional). When the body is overloaded with impressions, the brain does not have the judgement to process these experiences properly, and the solar plexus becomes blocked. It is similar to what happens at a busy junction when there are too many cars that do not follow the traffic regulations.

Prana (Vitality)

Before we are born we rely on the union with our mother via the umbilical cord. In the same way, after our birth, the same point unites with the consciousness of the Source which in Sanskrit is called *Brahma*. In order for the solar plexus to function as a continuous recipient of energy, it has to be purified. If it is not, it loses its ability to be "self-sufficient" and then has to achieve this with deep breaths and food.

We are what we eat, think, feel and experience, so if the food we eat or the difficult situations we may have, are hard to digest, then residues are created which eventually become toxic. These toxins make the body slower and more demanding.

The solar plexus works with the element of fire. This fire disperses both food and impressions and is called *agni*, the 'digestive fire'. The more powerful *agni* is, the easier it is to digest food and impressions. The main aim is to build a strong digestive system which can work quickly and effectively, without leaving any residue and without wasting our energy.

During the yoga sessions, we try not only to strengthen the digestive system but also to get rid of as many impressions as we can both from the present and also the past. By cleaning the system we can help the reprogramming of the body so that it can take as much food as is required and no more. We also encourage the mental programming of discrimination so that we can process our information, experiences and other stimuli correctly.

Although we should expect to have strong stomachs and clearer minds by doing this practice, the reality is that some participants (especially if it is their first time) might experience the opposite at the beginning. Your stomach may become more sensitive and confused and you may experience a bitter taste on your tongue. Your mind may become overloaded and you may have nonsensical dreams which result in waking up tired. This is due to the detoxification which is occurring, both to the physical body but also to the invisible ones. Those who repeat the programme, however, usually get through this stage more easily, and after a few classes manage to have strong stomachs and a good night's sleep.

Physical Exercise
Pawana Mukta Kriya - The gas releasing action
(From the Gitananda Yoga Tradition)

This is a wonderful practice which strengthens the stomach, frees trapped air and releases the tension which 'sits' in the solar plexus area. We use the leg and the breath to massage the stomach and liver. We use the sound '*Ha*!' for more intense psychological relief.

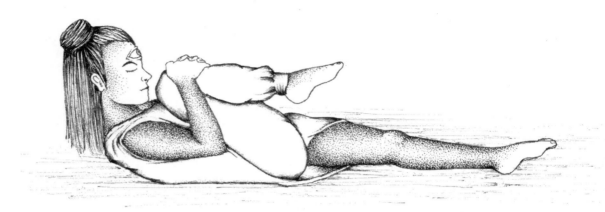

Start with you right leg. Breathe in (abdominal breathing) and try to get both your head and knee as close together as possible. Hold the position for 1-2 seconds and then kick out the leg as you exhale and shout out the sound '*ha*!'

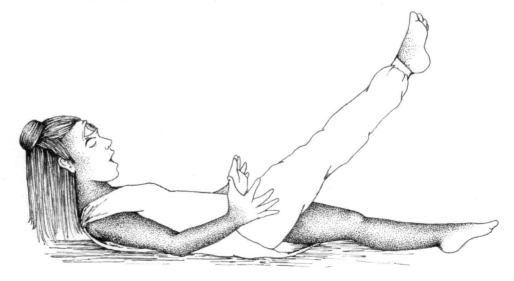

Repeat this 3 times and then do the same with the left leg.

Meditative Breathing
Yoga Nidraa - Charging of the Solar Plexus
(From the Gitananda Yoga Tradition)

Charge your body using the polarity breath for 9-27 rounds. Do not forget to use complete breathing and to breathe through the nose ONLY. On a chosen out-breath, bring your awareness from the feet to the belly button. Focus on a tiny spot, no bigger than the head of a pin, and start creating a circle around it, clockwise, which gets bigger and bigger, and continue doing this for 1-3 minutes. To ensure you do it correctly, imagine there is a clock on your belly. After that, continue creating a spiral which will eventually become so big that it goes around the whole body. Then close the spiral anti-clockwise and 'lock' it deep inside your body until it reaches the spinal cord. Focus on this for 1-3 minutes.

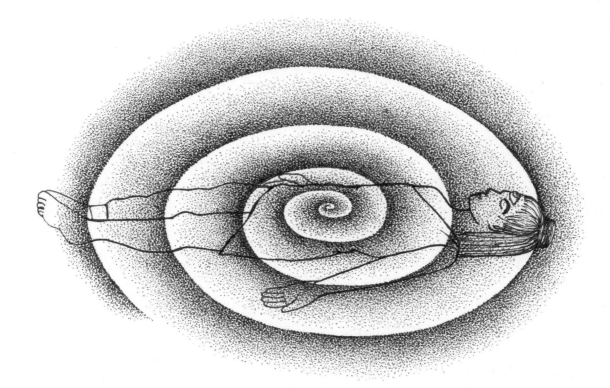

This exercise cleanses and charges the solar plexus. The spiral movement drives away unwanted impressions and simultaneously energises the whole body. The spiral shape strengthens the energy current. The closing of the spiral helps accumulate the energy back into the solar plexus when it is 'locked in'. This is an excellent exercise for therapists who tend to absorb negative energy from their patients.

Mental Exercise
Marmanasthanam Kriya (From the Gitananda Yoga Tradition)
& Cleansing of the Day
(From the book "Karma Manual" by Dr John Mumford)

The exercise below works in the same way as the spiral exercise, but more literally. We usually combine both (starting with the mental activity, followed by the charging of the solar plexus) for a complete intense cleaning. It should be done only at the end of the day and is ideal for a pleasant sound sleep as the mind consciously processes the information of the day, so it does not have to do it when we are sleeping. In this way we dream less - which is good because dreams waste a lot of mental energy - and there is also less tension during sleep.

At the end of the day, lie down or sit somewhere peaceful. Do a quick trip of the 22 parts of the body – *Marmanasthanam Kriya* (Gitananda Yoga). Just think about them, with no effort, in the following order:

1.   Toes
2.   Feet
3.   Calves
4.   Thighs
5.   Buttocks
6.   Tailbone
7.   Pelvis
8.   Belly
9.   Chest
10.   Shoulders
11.   Fingers
12.   Hands
13.   Hands to elbows
14.   Arms to shoulders
15.   Neck
16.   Mouth and chin
17.   Nose and cheeks
18.   Eyes
19.   Ears
20.   Back of the head
21.   Top of the head
22.   Space between the eyebrows

Then bring your awareness to your *chitakash*, the dark space in front of your closed eyes. This will be your screen where you will 'see' your day from the end (now) till the start (from the moment you woke up). It is important that you see your day backwards so the mind can 'unfold' the events accordingly.

We "Observe" our day:
A) Without judgement
B) Without excuses
C) Without commentary
...As if we were watching a movie.

The procedure explained above may take 4-8 minutes depending on how complicated your day was.

If you have watched a movie during the day or if you have read a book or magazine, it might be a good idea to remind yourself of it through this practice, because most of the 'mental rubbish' we have is created from such information (which is not ours!).

Be careful with this activity because at the start, the mind has a tendency to get tired and you may end up not finishing it at all. We hear a lot of snoring when we do this activity with the group...!

Life Practice
Change of Perspective - Detachment

The secret to a clean solar plexus – which gives us a strong character and a calmer life – is the practice of detachment. That is to see our life from a distance and not to relate what is occurring to us with our real existence. We are not our thoughts! We are not our thoughts! **We are not our thoughts!** What we are is something more than our thoughts. This is the tool that can awaken our discrimination. If we relate to what is happening around us, it is very hard to be uncritical and objective.

In order to install the programme of detachment into our systems, we first have to detach ourselves from... extreme joy. If we ask our brain to not feel sad with the tragedies that occur, it will see it as a threat to survival. If, on the other hand, we ask it not to be enthusiastic with pleasant things, this will not be seen as dangerous to the system and it will accept it. This is not the rejection of joy. On the contrary, it's the release of joy, but within us. Right now our joy depends on whether positive things will or will not happen to us. If something nice happens, we get excited for a while but when something unpleasant happens, the joy disappears. Is it not better for us to permanently have a more gentle form of joy, such as bliss for example. Then we do not have to wait for external factors to feel well.

Next time something nice happens to you, try to detach yourself from the event. If you can manage to not get too excited with the happy events, then you will not get so disappointed with the unpleasant ones either. Life is not just continuous joy, and it can never be, but it can have continuous serenity if we train our minds to think in this way.

"He who is not attached, who is not affected either by pleasant or unpleasant events, has a stable mind."

(Bhagavad Gita)

Weeks 7-9
Second Major Consumer: Pelvis
Area of the body: Pelvis and the Sacrum

The pelvic area represents the feeling of pleasure. This pleasure is usually connected to food, sex and our general wellbeing. Many thousands of years ago when human conscience became weak and could not distinguish which of its actions were harmful, religious and social laws were introduced to restore security. Since then, people have become somewhat confused regarding the extent of pleasure they should have. So now, they either enjoy too much pleasure (which some consider unethical) or suppress it altogether (which can lead to guilt). The pelvis, which was initially a holy part of the body and the 'store room' of vitality, is now overloaded with feelings of guilt.

These three weeks are more concerned with cleaning the pelvic area of these impressions rather than recharging it. We shall return to the pelvic area in a few months though so we can charge and 'fill' it. In the more advanced practices which are not covered in this book, we also return to it one more time for a final charging of the pelvic area. If one has followed the practices from the beginning and has made an effort to perfect them, then they know that the final charging of the pelvis can also be transferred successfully to the brain. This can only happen if one also follows the life practices, however.

Physical Exercise
Namaskarasana - Salutation Posture
(From the Satyananda Yoga Tradition and the Shakti Bandha)

Sit deeply as shown in the picture. As you breathe in (complete breathing) open your legs and the trunk of your body. As you breathe out, close your legs and stretch your arms forward. (As shown below). Do this 3 times, coordinating it with your breath; then stay in the open position and do a few breaths, then close and stay in this position for a few breaths. In the closed pose it is better to do shallow abdominal breathing only.

This exercise helps to open the pelvic area and to release impressions and blockages from there.

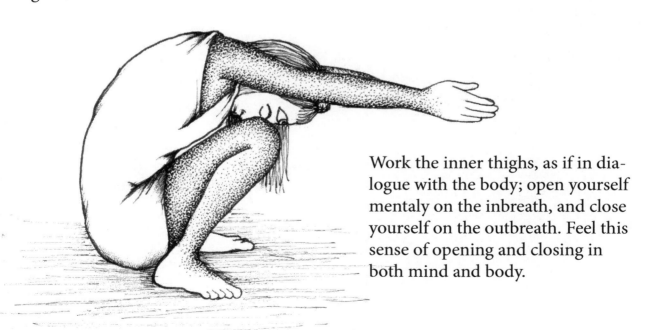

Work the inner thighs, as if in dialogue with the body; open yourself mentaly on the inbreath, and close yourself on the outbreath. Feel this sense of opening and closing in both mind and body.

49

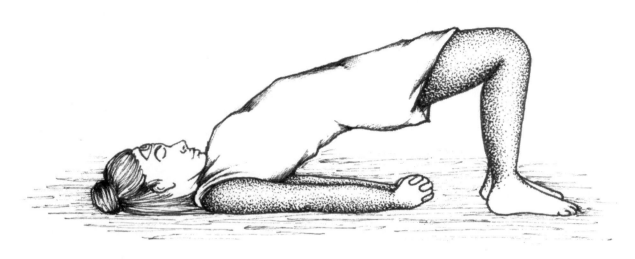

Alternative Exercise - *Sethu Asana*

If you find the previous posture challenging, then an alternative is the bridge posture (*Sethu Asana*). Keep your legs as wide apart as possible. At this point imagine that the tailbone is a long pencil and try to 'draw' circles with it on the wall opposite you (i.e. make circular movements with your pelvis). Don't worry too much about how the body is moving, just imagine the circle on the wall. Breathe in and move towards the right, breathe out and move towards the left. After 6-9 repetitions, remain in the *sethu asana* position for about 20-30 seconds stretching the pelvis upwards as much as you can.

Meditative Breathing
Charging/Cleansing of the pelvis.

Lie on your back (*Shava Asana, p.32*) with your head facing north.
Start with the polarity breath. (*Anu Loma Viloma Pranayama*).

After 9-27 rounds of breathing and visualisation, use your last out-breath to take you as far as the pelvis only (not all the way up) and move the breath first towards the left of the pelvis using the colour blue, and then, breathing in towards the right using the colour red. Using your awareness, continue going right and left over the pelvis in this way.

Feel the movement of prana with your breath and understand how the brain can move this prana wherever it wants within the body. The prana is the energy force, the breath is the vehicle and the mind is the driver of this vehicle. Guide your breath so it can 'brush over' and cleanse the pelvis. Start with a rhythm of 6:6 (breathe in for 6, breathe out for 6) and then continue with 4:4, 2:2. 1:1, remembering to guide the brain to the right when you inhale using the colour red and to the left when you exhale using the colour blue. Do at least nine rounds each time with each rhythm. Then breathe normally and let the breath move as fast as you can from right (red) to left (blue) for 1-3 minutes.

Please note: *use complete breathing until the 4:4 rhythm, but then use only abdominal breathing for the other parts.*

Mental Exercise
The Vessel with the Holy Liquid

Imagine that the pelvis is a vessel (*in Sanskrit, the pelvis is known as 'the vessel which contains holy fluid', and in Greek, the back bone of the pelvis is known as the 'holy bone'*). Imagine that this vessel is connected to the brain via the spinal cord. Contemplate this connection. Whatever is happening to the pelvis is also happening to the brain - not just physically but hormonally (the reproductive system is designed to have lots of connections with the brain). It is very important to **FEEL THIS CONNECTION.**

An extension to this exercise: the next time that you feel that the pelvis is very full, imagine that the area is on fire. Then visualise that due to the heat, a clear gas is being created instead of smoke, which goes through the spine to the brain. This gas, which is very refined and contains light, fills and energises the brain.

Life Practice
The Creative Energy

During these practices it is a good idea to experiment with your sexual energy. It is a great opportunity to realise that sexual energy is in actual fact concentrated energy (*prana*). This concentrated energy is also referred to by some as *Kundalini*. This means that sexual energy does not necessarily have to be released during sexual activity; it can also be directed towards our higher energy centers. Sexual energy is simply our creative energy.

In yoga there are many techniques that can channel the energy far higher (once it has been produced and conserved). *Kriya* yoga is especially concentrated on the control and channelling of prana towards the brain. The modern western world however, has misunderstood these techniques, has used them in the wrong way and has created a massive cloud of illusions around them which does not accomplish anything.

Therefore, at first, we may need to experiment so that we can become aware that sexual energy does not always mean the sexual act and release. This awareness has to happen simply, slowly and without pressure. Start to experiment with your sexual energy. Try to realise when the pelvis is full of prana – in other words, when it is stimulated. When the pelvis is extremely full with prana, then it has a desperate need for sexual expression. In our days, this happens quite fast since there are sexually stimulating messages everywhere. Sometimes though, the need for sexual expression comes without a full pelvis, because of habit or a sense of duty. In such cases, the sexual act drains the creative energy. Those who want to use this creative energy for spiritual reasons, have to learn to acknowledge this and try to avoid it. The sexual act should only occur when both partners are 'full'. There is nothing wrong with the sexual act itself. In the same way that it is not wrong for someone who has money to buy an expensive item for himself, it is also not wrong to be sexually liberated, giving pleasure and love. If however we abuse this creative energy with excessive sexual activity, it can only be compared to a poor person getting a loan to buy an expensive car without knowing how to ever repay it.

We have to note however, that it is not just too much sexual activity that drains creative energy. It is all the 'major consumers': indigestion, hunger, anger, need for dominance, emotional pressure, unnecessary and senseless talking, sexual oppression etc.

Food for Thought
The pelvis is 'full' with clear creative energy when:
1.   We can feel a light vibration
2.   We can feel slight electricity
3.   We feel a sense of pleasure or completeness in that area
4.   We feel mentally strong and focused
5.   We feel invincible
6.   We feel sexually stimulated
7.   ...Lots more, since each person experiences it differently.

Weeks 10-12
Third Major Consumer: Relationships

During this period, if any new members join our group, they either think that they are experiencing a 'new kind' of yoga, or that they are visiting a mental institution...! In essence, what we are trying to do in this period is to release the pressure that has accumulated due to the social rules that govern our lives.

Society has allowed us to develop and live safely (at least from our environment). However, our animal nature lives within us, but because it is suppressed it tries to find small windows of expression: hooliganism, hunting, violent movies and gossip are just some examples of this.

All of this is created by the oppressed animal instinct which has been distorted by the laws of survival. If a person does not 'filter' the socially unacceptable expressions, he is considered insane. In fact, the difference between a 'sane' and an insane person is that the former can suppress his spontaneous actions whereas the latter, for some reason, cannot.

The 'sensible ones' amongst us however pay the price. They may not be locked in institutions, but they may end up in hospitals with psychosomatic illnesses. How many times have we wanted to shout, to disagree, to cry out loud, to do something erratic or to simply say 'no' but we haven't done so because it is not polite or acceptable. All these suppress actions, which if are not freed, stay within our bodies and create a blockage - and eventually the body gets sick. Some of us may find ways to express ourselves through extreme sports or an eccentric hobby. Others have psychotherapy sessions. These are all effective. With yoga however, the release of suppressed actions occurs through awareness: the yogi does not wait for his meeting with his psychoanalyst to search within himself and to express himself. The yogi uses a 24 hour awareness programme, and in this way, releases any suppressed actions immediately before they are stored in the body.

Our job within the next three weeks is to become free of as many suppressed actions as we can using:
A) Sound
B) Physical Action
C) Visualisation

When we start to feel 'lighter' we will be in a position to understand when a certain action has been suppressed and then can get rid of it immediately. We analyse the situation immediately, just like a psychoanalyst would, without complications and delays. The fresher the event the easier it is for it to go. Actually, what we need is to learn to train ourselves to analyse the events of our lives faster so that we can be free from them as early as possible.

"Analysis brings Solution"

Physical Exercise
Emptying

Lie on your back (*shava asana*, p.32). Breathe in and lift your legs, arms, head and shoulders in the air and shake them making any kind of sound you want until your breath runs out. Then stop and 'throw' your body to the ground and stay still for a few seconds. Repeat this many times until you feel you cannot do it anymore. And just when you feel you cannot do another one, do one more and then release your body on the floor again, this time for three minutes. You will feel an amazing rush in your body after this exercise. You can then spread this rush mentally to your whole body and especially to your limbs and genital area. Then the rush will disappear and will be replaced with a feeling of deep relaxation which will also be spread over the whole body.

Meditative Breathing
Brahma Mudra
(From the Gitananda Yoga Tradition)

This practice is a wonderful way to combine movement with breath and sound. It is a complicated practice which needs to be repeated many times to become perfect. It is an opportunity for all to 'feel' the sound instead of purely hearing it. Only when we can *feel* sound can it enter our cells, and only then can we experience the power of words. Then, as we become sensitive to words, words will have more power in our lives.

When we use sound, it would be a good idea for the rhythm of our breath to be

56

1:3. In other words, our outbreath should last three times as long as our inbreath. This is actually very difficult for many people to do so during the group practices I prefer the 1:2 rhythm. Usually we inhale with a count of 6 and exhale with a count of 12.

Sit in any meditative position with a straight back, facing north, or looking towards the north. Join the fingers of both your hands using *Yoga Mudra*.

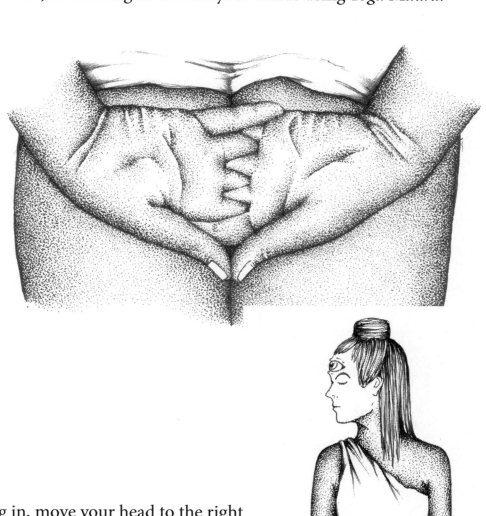

Breathing in, move your head to the right counting to 6, and then breathing out move your head back to the middle counting to 12, making the continuous sound '*ahhhh....*' as you do so.

Then breathing in move your head to the left counting to 6, and breathing out move your head back to the middle counting to 12, making the continuous sound *'Ooooh...'* as you do so.

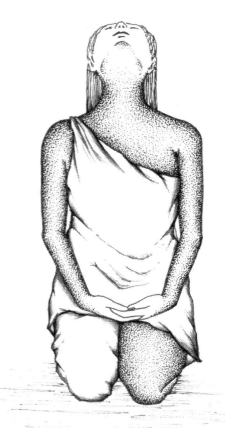

After that, move your head upwards (6) as you breathe in, then bring your head back to the middle (12) with the sound *'Eeeeeee...'* as you do so.

Finally, breathe in and move your head downwards so that your chin reaches the base of your neck (6) and breathe out bringing your head back to the middle (12) making the sound *'mmm'* as you do so.

This is one round. Do nine rounds.

Mental Exercise
Cleansing with Sound

Lie down in the Shava Asana position or sit in any meditative position with a straight back. Do a quick journey of the 22 parts of the body (*Marmanasthanam Kriya*). Then feel the shape of your body. Start trying to 'empty' your body until it becomes hollow. The body becomes an empty mould with the shape of your body. Feel and visualise that your body is completely empty and then start to make a low, light *'mmmmmm'* sound and try to feel that the sound is traveling around and vibrating in your empty body. Think of what happens when you talk in an empty room. The sound cannot be absorbed so it reverberates from one wall to another. Allow the vibration of the sound to shake your body so that it will clean it. You can also repeat the sound *'ommm'* mentally using the same visualisation.

Life Practice
Sound as Vibration/ Meaningful Relationships

Although we live in the period of 'expression', it is still a good idea to experiment first with sounds and then with relationships. I recommend attending a live classical music concert if possible, and instead of just listening to the music, attempt to feel the vibration of the live sound in your spinal cord. Another idea is to meditate in the countryside and to feel the sounds of nature before the mind has a chance to interpret them; in other words, to feel the sounds of nature as if we do not know what each one is and to allow them to vibrate. Only when we become more sensitive to the vibration of sound through this practice, can we feel what meaningless conversation and meaningless relationships do to our bodies.

Relationships are the most difficult part of the practice. This is why I make statements in the form of questions, so that each one can decide whether to simply answer the questions or to act upon them.
Ask yourselves daily:

1. Out of all the people I met today, how many did I really want to spend time with?
2. How many times did I do something today that I did not want to do because of someone else?
3. Regarding the people I met today, how many did I really want to see and how many did I see because I had to or out of habit?
4. How many times today did I do something for the approval of others, or

did I not do something for fear of being criticized?

5. Did I stay on my own at all? How happy was I being alone?

6. How many times was it necessary for me to speak and how many times did I speak just so there would not be silence?

7. How many times today did I hear something interesting which was also useful? How many times did I simply listen to others passively or listen because it would have been rude to interrupt?

These realisations will prepare us to perfect the three-fold communication (Solitude/ companionship/ social life) which we will refer to in the throat chakra.

Life Practice 2
Mauna (Silence)

Mauna is a spiritual practice which is quite common in some religions and spiritual methods. During mauna we abstain from any type of communication with the aim of charging and internalising and for self-inquiry. It is an excellent practice which clears the mind and brings our real selves to the surface.

Although it may look like we are going against our very selves (since we would really like to speak and we have to suppress ourselves), in actual fact we are allowing forgotten and more real parts of us to bloom and express themselves. This happens because we are consciously recycling within us all those words that we would have released, and this creates an amazing current of energy which 'burns' our regular impressions. When our regular impressions are cleared, new hidden impressions appear in our conscious mind from our subconscious mind.
Speaking, unfortunately, is an overused practice and words are so distorted that they do not serve any purpose in self-expression – instead they simply satisfy our social existence.

Mauna can be practiced in three ways and can last from one hour to many days. One suggestion is to choose one day in the month and apply one of the following three mauna methods for 24 hours:

1. Complete isolation and silence (no meetings, phones, emails, newspapers, TV, internet etc.).
2. Silence in our daily relationships (if there is a practical need, then communication should be in written form only)
3. Speaking, but with one of the following limitations:

a) Limit the amount of times we speak. We decide from the beginning of the day, how many times we will speak and only if it is absolutely necessary (you will be surprised at how few times we really *need* to speak).

or

b) We speak normally, but without using the words 'I', 'you', 'we', 'yes', 'no' and only when our words are not excuses, comments, analysis or judgements.

Weeks 13-15

Standing Postures - Strengthening/Exercising the mind

Certainly the ancient yogis did not create the standing postures with the intention of strengthening their arms and their legs, or to tighten their buttocks. They must have had something else in mind when they prudently stood motionless in the warrior pose or the triangle pose. At first I would quickly bypass these standing exercises because they reminded me of the gym. Since these postures are considered some of the strongest ones, they are very popular with those who want to use Yoga as a workout. However, I slowly discovered that the standing postures can work more effectively on the mind than the body, if used with awareness.

When we assume these postures, we always need to be aware of the shape that our body takes each time. And, so that we do not forget the mind, we visualise the shape of each posture and we follow it up with our breath. At the start, everyone does these exercises rather superficially, or they concentrate more on how to bend or twist correctly so they can be more flexible. However, when I ask for better alignment of these postures and not just to 'do' these postures but to 'become' them, then their bodies are transformed. In the end, even those who do not have the power or flexibility to do them 'correctly', eventually manage to create beautiful postures and can concentrate on them better.

Physical Exercise
Trikona Asana - The Tringle Posture

This is an ancient and very powerful pose which activates the prana within the body if used for this purpose. In essence we create a type of pyramid with our body – we become a pyramid. Whether the hand that touches the floor remains closed (a fist) or whether we keep the hand somewhere on our bodies, this connection creates energy that is 'recycled' by flowing through the triangle, and this makes us stronger. Feel the triangle that you have formed with your body.

Meditative Breathing
Mental Massage

(From the system: *Vibrational Breath Therapy - VBT*)

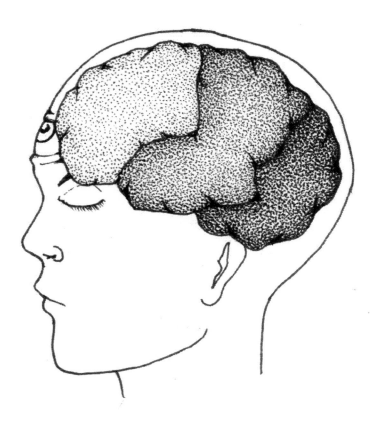

Visualise the three parts of the brain:
1. The back part (reptilian brain)
2. The sides of the brain (mammalian brain)
3. The front of the brain (neocortex)

Try to connect the back part with the lower part of the lungs, the sides of the brain with the middle part of the lungs and the front part of the brain with the upper part of our lungs. As you are doing complete breathing for this, think about the back, sides and front of the brain. Connect the lungs with the different parts of the brain to the point that you feel that the lungs *are* the brain and that you are breathing with your brain. This practice functions as a 'mental massage' of the brain and activates all three parts of the brain equally. Do this practice from 9 to 27 times with awareness: inhale, starting with the back, moving to the sides and then the front of the brain, and then exhale in the same way (back, sides, front).

'Yoga creates bridges between the three brains of the genetic development of human beings in such a way that they can go beyond their animal instinct and claim a place next to God'.
Yoga Maharish Dr Swami Gitananda

Mental Exercise
The Transcendental Mind

Now is the time to 'open' our mind and to focus on things whose 'form' we may not be familiar with. This will encourage the brain to improvise and to use all its inners senses, not only the more familiar 'inner sight'. We usually 'see' dreams, forgetting that in our dreams we can smell things, hear sounds/words too. Or, on many occasions, our dreams are simply a feeling that does not identify with any of the five senses. There are people who believe they cannot receive messages from higher dimensions because they do not have a strong inner sight or inner hearing. There is great confusion regarding this, so this exercise helps us find which of our inner senses is stronger and to use it in order to communicate with the higher source. There are many levels of this exercise, from the beginner to the advanced level.

When we do this exercise we should remain at each stage for 1-3 minutes and then move on the next one.

- Lie down on your back *(shava asana)*. Focus on the atmosphere in the room (sound, smells, feelings etc).

- Now feel a sense of warmth which is being emitted from your body, a few centimetres around the body.

- Feel the shape of the body.

- Go into your body, and feel that it is motionless. The internal organs continue to function as normal: the heart is beating, the blood is flowing, the stomach is digesting, the bowels are moving the food, the glands are secreting liquids/hormones etc.

- Now move even further into your bodies and feel the cells of your body vibrating. Note how the vibration changes depending on your thoughts.

- Within the next three minutes move your awareness to the organs that are functioning within your body, to the shape of your body, then then warmth that your body is emitting and eventually back to the environment in the room. Move your hands and your feet and complete the practice.

There is a more creative variation that can be done in an upright position (with closed eyes):

- Focus on the environment in the room (sounds, smells, atmosphere etc).

- Now feel a sense of warmth which is emitted from your body, a few centimetres around the body.

- Feel the shape of the body.

- Go into your body, and feel that it is motionless. The internal organs continue to function moving the food as normal: the heart is beating, the blood is flowing, the stomach is digesting, the bowels are moving the food, the glands are secreting liquids/hormones etc.

- Now imagine that your internal organs are musical instruments that are working together to create music. Listen to the music that the instruments are making.

- Imagine that the music within you is producing a very strong, clear light in your inner body.

- This light is so intense that it eventually escapes from the body and surrounds it. You continue to feel the music. If you feel it, then you can move a little with the rhythm of this inner music.

- The light now expands and fills the room. The music can be heard outside the body.

- The music and the light come out of the body and fill the town, country, world.

- We allow the light and the music to expand as much as we want, and then we revert; we feel our bodies, we move our fingers and toes and complete the exercise.

Life Practice
Unimportant Importance

Our aim in this period is to 'expand' the mind. A good way to do this is to see things, situations, people in a different way. Use your senses: feel the smells and realise how much they influence you. Absorb the sunset with your eyes. Listen to and enjoy your favourite sounds. Start to feel the vibes a certain space gives you, and do not remain in spaces that do not make you feel good (or try to change the energy of that space with your mind; in this way you can help others too).
My favourite exercise is called 'Unimportant Importance'. We go to a public place and we find unimportant details which can become important if we give them attention: the glimpse of a passer-by, a leaf that falls off the tree, the shapes of the buildings and the road etc.
Life is never boring when we approach it with awareness.

Weeks 16-18
The Sacrum / The Holy Vessel
LOMA-VILOMA Practices (From the *Gitananda Yoga* Tradition)

Following the cleansing' of the pelvis and the holy sacrum which we covered during weeks 7-9, we shall now continue by 'filling' this vessel, using two opposite energies which flow within our bodies. *Loma* represents the male (warm energy) and *Viloma* represents the female (cold energy). Both energies flow in both male and female bodies. The aim of this *Loma-Viloma* practice is to find the correct balance between these 2 energies in order to create polarity (a healthy charging of the electromagnetic field). This has no connection with 'manliness' and 'femininity'; with this practice, polarity will strengthen the best traits of both genders.

With polarity, the system receives the most intense charging of the electromagnetic field. This charging is 'stored' at the sacrum, our holy vessel. Some may describe this charging as 'divine energy'. Divine energy is very similar to sexual energy since the "divine quality" is very similar to the feeling of having an orgasm, but it is much more intense. It is therefore understandable why so many people get addicted to sex, since it is so similar to divine sensations! The aim of the yogi is to manage to refine this divine energy and to use it to charge the mind.

This series of practices of *Loma-Viloma* make us understand and learn how to produce and save this 'divine' energy in our pelvis, through:

1. **Asanas/postures:** the "waterfall effect" – to create angles, preferably vertical, with our body, using gravity to increase the flow of blood and energy to the pelvis.
2. **Visualisations:** so you can keep your minds on the pelvis in order to help it charge. The visualisations are: On the the in-breath, move towards the right within the pelvis with a red colour and then on the out-breath move towards the left within the pelvis using the colour blue.
3. **Breathing:** Complete breathing through the nose, in order to create the maximum positive charging with the inbreath and the maximum negative charging with the outbreath. When you consciously create equal positive and negative charging, you produce electromagnetic energy which can be directed with the visualisation at the pelvis.

What we are actually doing for more than an hour, is an active meditation, focusing mind, body and breath on the pelvis.

Physical Exercise
Nava Asana - The Boat Posture

With this posture, we form an angle with our torso and legs, focusing on the pelvis. The circulation of the blood increases at the pelvis as does the charging of energy. At the exact point where the legs and torso make the angle, visualise a wave of red light passing over, moving towards the right as you breathe in and a wave of blue light moving towards the left as you breathe out. In this way, you have your awareness at the pelvis while blood flows to it, resulting in it being charged positively (*loma*) and negatively (*viloma*), producing electricity/vitality.

Wherever the blood flows, prana goes.
Wherever the mind goes, prana follows.
Prana = vitality = charging = electricity.

Meditative Breathing
Aloma-Viloma Pranayama - Alternate Nostril Breathing
(From the Gitananda Yoga Tradition)

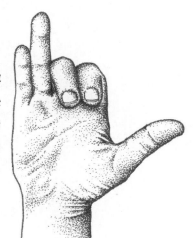

Nasarga Mudra
We shall use *Nasarga Mudra* in order to close one nostril at every inbreath/outbreath. We use the right thumb to close the right nostril and the ring finger to close the left nostril.

The rhythm of the breath is:
6:3:6:3 *(breathe in 6 seconds, hold your breath for 3 seconds; breathe out 6 seconds, hold your breath for 3 seconds)*
Or
8:4:8:4 *(breathe in 8 seconds, hold your breath for 4 seconds: breathe out 8 seconds, hold your breath for 4 seconds)*

Sit in a comfortable meditative position with a straight back, looking towards the north.
Close your left nostril with your middle finger and take a complete breath from the right nostril.
Hold your breath.
Then hold your right nostril with your thumb and breathe out from the left nostril.
Hold your breath.
Then breathe in from your left.
Hold your breath.
Close your left nostril and breathe out from the right nostril.
Hold your breath.

This is one round. Do 9 or 18 or 27 rounds.

Then, sit quietly for a few moments in *Antar Mouna* (inner silence).
This practice charges the nervous system uniformly, stimulating both the right and left hemispheres of the brain equally. In this way the charging which is created in the pelvis, is somehow 'neutralised' and can be used for higher mental practices.

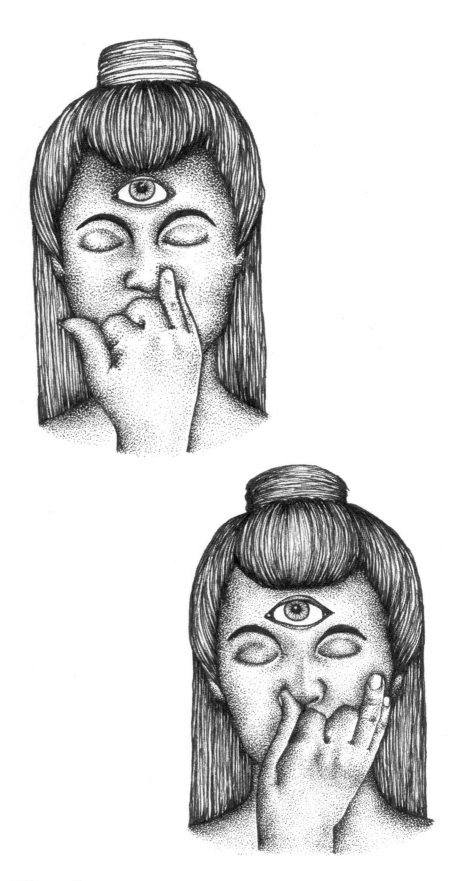

Aloma - Viloma Pranayama

Mental Exercise
Tuning with Higher Frequencies

After the exercises we sit quietly in *Antar Mouna* (inner silence) and concentrate on the high notes of the Tibetan singing bowl, or we concentrate on classical music: (Vivaldi's four Seasons is an ideal choice) or opera with lots of high notes. We have to feel the music in our spinal cord rather than just listen to it. This converts the energy from physical to higher mental or spiritual. Allow the energy to flow and 'store' the sensation of 'creative serenity' in a way that you can recall it whenever it is needed in your life.

Life Practice
Guiding the Creative Energy

Now is the time, since you have built creative energy with these practices, to learn how to manage it. During weeks 7-9 you were taught to feel when you are 'full', and how this does not necessarily mean sexuality and its release. Its control (and not its suppression) is a very difficult thing which might take many years to perfect. **It is difficult to transcend sexuality because we don't know what to replace it with.** So if you find a different way of using this creative energy, then it will not be automatically transformed into something sexual. If, on the other hand, you choose sexual expression, the energy will become more dynamic and more creative than ever.

The guidance of creative energy is not an exercise we do with the group. It is a practice which occurs in our lives, until we save it as programming, so that we can then consciously choose how to use our creative energy:

1. For personal physical therapy, by holding the inbreath and guiding the energy from the pelvis to the place where the therapy is required.
2. To solve problems, for creativity, for better concentration, for meditation. Hold the out breath and imagine that an empty space is created within the spine which automatically pulls the energy inside of the spinal cord to the brain. Lock this energy in the brain by giving it a spiral shape.
3. For prayer or for a service towards others, connect the pelvis with the heart using the in-breath.
4. For strength and energy (sexual or physical), connect the pelvis with the solar plexus using the in-breath.

5. For the release of sexual tension if this is causing discomfort - use the outbreath so you can send energy from the pelvis to the genitals and from there to the legs (inner thighs) so that it can exit from the feet (the feet must be firmly on the ground).

All the above apply to those who have worked with the cleansing techniques in the previous lessons. If the energy at the pelvis is impure, it cannot be converted and channelled.

Sometimes the group is very tired after the physical exercises of *Loma Viloma*. If this happens, it means that the practice is cleansing instead of charging the system. The best solution in such cases is sleep. Utilise this period to sleep a little more to allow the energy channels to be cleansed of old tension that may exist.

Other members have the opposite results: hypertension, increased appetite, hyperactivity. If you can control it then all is well; if you lose control however then this means that the nervous system was charged more than it should have been. Maintain contact with the 5 elements in their natural forms (air in the mountains, sea, lake, river, soil, gardening, sun, sky) but especially contact with the earth, in order to relax the nervous system.

For those who have charged the system with the previous practices, the result will be 'creative serenity'.

Chakras
Energy Centers

After the cleansing period that lasts from September to December we start work on the energy centres – the *Chakras*.

The *chakras* are concentrated energy centres which are responsible for the collection and the conversion of *Prana* (vital energy) for our physical, emotional, mental and spiritual needs. The *Chakras* 'digest' the most refined food of all – *Prana*. In some yoga traditions, the *chakras* represent the elements from which we are made: earth (first *chakra*), water (second *chakra*), fire (third *chakra*), air (fourth *chakra*), ether (fifth *chakra*) and mind (sixth *chakra*). The *chakras* are connected to specific points of the spinal cord and specific hormonal glands and nervous plexuses, but they are not located there. We can influence the chakras depending on how we use the body, but the most common form of influence is via our repetitive thoughts and actions. Our thoughts and actions can affect our hormonal glands just as much as the glands can affect them. It is a reciprocal relationship. Any work done with meditation, yoga, healing of energy centres, etc. has to be in conjunction with life practice – otherwise the result is temporary and creates many illusions.

When working with the *chakras* we use a physical posture (*asana*) which lasts from 1 to 3 minutes. At the same time, we visualise the element/quality that each *chakra* represents. This affects:
1. The part of the spinal cord which is connected to the *Chakra*
2. The part of the body and the internal organs/nervous plexus which is connected to the *Chakra*
3. The hormonal gland which is connected to the *Chakra*

This is followed by a meditative breathing technique, a mental exercise and a life practice which work with the psychological qualities of each *chakra*.

The table below describes everything that is covered regarding each *chakra*. The *chakra* points of the body/spinal cord/glands are from the Gitananda Yoga tradition. Other yoga traditions vary a little.

CHAKRAS AND THEIR QUALITIES/ CHAKRA VISUALISATIONS

CHAKRA	Part of the Spine	Part of the Body/ Internal Organs	Hormonal Gland	Element/ Image for Visualisation/ Quality	People in our lives who are connected with the quality of the chakra
1.Muladhara	Tailbone	Genitals	Testes/Ovaries	Earth/Roots/ Safety	Parents
2.Swadhisthana	Sacrum	Intestines/ Kidneys	Adrenal Glands	Water/ Running water/ Flexibility	Lovers
3.Manipura	Thoracic (T12)	Stomach	Pancreas	Fire/ Golden Sun/ Action	People we feel impose on us, or vice versa
4.Anahata	Thoracic (T5)	Heart	Thymus Gland	Air/Flower/ Unity	Our most loved one
5.Vishuddhi	Cervical (C3)	Throat/ Vocal Chords	Thyroid Gland	Ether/Sky/ Self-expression	Our true self
6.Ajna	Center of the Brain	Brain	Pituitary Gland	Mind/ Pinecone or Eye/ Higher knowledge	Our higher self or spiritual teacher

Chakras - The Three-Part Practice

The *Chakra* practice is divided into three parts:

1. Cleansing of the first, second and third *Chakras*

The first three *Chakras* are where our brain saves whatever has eclipsed our consciousness: traumas, complexes, desires, obstacles etc. When these are cleared through self-awareness, then these three energy centres express higher forms of our consciousness, and, most importantly, open the path for vitality to nourish the three higher energy centres, which contain (in deactivated form) the higher qualities of human existence: empathy, love, clear communication, truth, the essence of the inseperable, telepathy, wisdom.

Think of it like this: our real existence obtains its strength from the vitality that each person carries and is followed by a path which leads to enlightenment – true knowledge. This path begins at the tail bone (first energy centre) and ends at a place higher/further than our head (the seventh energy centre) - or even more accurately, ends in infinity. If the first energy centres have hoarded memories, thoughts and fears, then our real existence is 'blinded' and cannot continue the path towards enlightenment. The need to purify is part of our existence which is why in every period of every civilisation there is at least one way to cleanse/purify: ecstatic dances, ceremonies, hymns, confession, psychoanalysis etc.

All of these are practical systems of cleansing and self-awareness which have the intention of 'opening' the path to the higher centre. When we eventually 'clean' these areas where the distortions exist, then our real existence can reach the higher energy levels and nourish them with vitality so they can activate our higher qualities.

If we rush to feed the higher centres with vitality without cleaning the lower ones first however, then the supposed enlightenment will be distorted with our personal memories. We will not be able to see the truth as it is, but will only see whatever suits our personal needs. **This is why during the training, three quarters of our practice is devoted to cleansing/purification.** This cleansing is not something that happens just once or twice, **but continues for the rest of our lives.** Each time, we clean another level, a different layer. This method makes the journey longer but more certain.

2. Activation of the fourth, fifth and sixth *Chakras*

Once we have passed our consciousness through the first three *Chakras* and we have awareness that for as long as we view reality through our 'layers', the real truth cannot be expressed, we will try to 'awaken' the higher energy centres. The physical exercises are not so important here, as the visualisations and mental exercises are the ones that directly affect the higher energy channels.

3. Activation of the seventh *Chakra* (which is not presented in this book)
This is the *Kriya Yoga* and *Mantra Laya* technique. We work all the *Chakras* physically with asanas, mentally with visualisations and symbols, emotionally by directing our breath, and verbally with mantras, thus opening the path to the mind and to the seventh energy centre.

The "Ideal Place" Visualisation, and Self-Healing

A very important tool that we use in our training with the *Chakras* is the self-healing that we carry out through the 'Ideal Place' visualisation. This 'place' is a location where we feel comfortable, safe and relaxed. We use it for visualisations without needing to actually be there physically. It might be a real place, or we can create one using our imagination; It can be an outdoor space (mountain, beach, valley, forest etc) or an indoor space (home, palace, temple, room etc). Once we have decided on the image and the atmosphere that will prevail at our ideal place, and have established that it is our safe haven, then we can 'bring' people from our lives who connect with the psychological quality of each *Chakra*. The purpose is to solve karmic and psychological ties with those who delay our process of cleansing and development. Our connections with friends, relatives, partners, colleagues and acquaintances is the main purpose of our incarnation. If the ego dominates in these relationships however, then the proper procedure for our development is hindered and these relationships create karma instead of purification. Detachment is key to the solution of these problems. With human relationships, however, there is a fine line regarding the limits between detachment and attachment. **We need to be able to come as close as is necessary, with the right people, who may change at any given moment.** The "Ideal Place" practice, detaches us symbolically from our conscious or unconscious attachments or conflicts with people, so that our relationships will serve our development. This is why it is very important to consciously choose the right people to bring to our ideal place, in addition to letting them go at the end of the practice.

Weeks 19-21
First Energy Center: Muladhara chakra (roots)

MULADHARA CHAKRA

Tailbone
Part of the body: **Genitals**
Element: **Earth**
Hormonal glands: **Testes/Ovaries**
It converts prana for: **Grounding, Stability, Safety, Strength** *(which stems from self-confidence)*
It is blocked by: **Fear**

The first energy centre and its qualities are formed very early in life – in the first seven years in fact, and those responsible for the sense of self-confidence are mainly our biological parents. Subconsciously, we connect the confidence that we have or don't have about ourselves with our parents.

During the asanas (physical postures), our awareness should be on the tailbone, which we visualise to be growing roots that are directed down into the ground with each exhale. This visualisation will balance the element of the earth in our system, grounding and stabilising us.

Physical Exercise
Kurma Asana - The Turtle Pose

We use forward bends to stimulate the first *Chakra*. Stay in this position for 1-3 minutes. The soles of your feet are connected and your hands are touching your feet. Ideally, the top of your head will also be touching your feet.

Breathe rhythmically (*breathe in 4 seconds, breathe out 4 seconds*) and every time you breathe out, imagine that the tailbone is a root that grows deeper and deeper into the ground.

Meditative Breathing
Rooting

Sit in a comfortable meditative position with your spinal cord straight, facing the north.

Practice complete rhythmic breathing (*breathe in 6, breathe out 6*) for ten minutes. With every out-breath, imagine that your tailbone is growing roots that are going deeper and wider into the ground. After that, devote 3-5 minutes on concentrating on the roots you have grown. What is their shape? How deep are they? How wide are they? Do they have a specific colour? Try to feel your roots.

Now try to feel that every time you inhale you gain strength from the earth and every time you exhale you give all your tension, traumas and worries to the earth. The earth will transform your 'rubbish' into fertiliser. Continue with this mental activity until you feel strong and clean.

When this practice is repeated a few times, it is as if we are installing the programming of stability/safety/strength, by using the symbol of the root. When the programming is installed, then we will need only 9 breaths whenever we feel we need it, for grounding ourselves, cleansing ourselves or re-establishing our power and self-confidence.

Mental Exercise
Energetic Detachment from our Parents

Part 1 - The Ideal Place
(To be practiced 3-9 times before progressing to part 2)

Lie on your back (*Shava Asana, p.32*) or sit in a position with your back straight.

Carry out a quick scan of the 22 body parts (*Marmanasthanam Kriya, p.45*) and then concentrate on your *Chittakash* (the dark place in front of your closed eyes). This will be your mental screen.

Watch yourself passing through an open market. A lot of people around you are talking, shouting, moving. Many of them are trying to get your attention: to show you something, to sell you something, to tell you something. They are people that you know (friends, relatives, acquaintances) and people you don't know. You look at them, but you do not stop. You continue to move through the market with the intention of leaving it behind.

Eventually, the road becomes steeper and you are slowly moving out of the market. You keep on walking, distancing yourself from the market. You keep walking upwards towards a hill. When you are the top of the hill, you are all alone. You can hear the noise from the marketplace but you are far from it. Now that you are alone at the top of the hill you look for your 'ideal place', you see it, and you go and sit there.

Try to envision a serene place which makes you feel good, and visualise it in detail on your mental screen. It can be a real place or it can be a place that you have

81

imagined, as long as it is somewhere that makes you feel comfortable and safe. Visualise yourself there, alone, sitting as you are sitting now. Experience it using all the senses: listen to the sounds around you, enjoy your surroundings, smell the smells, feel the place with your body, experience the atmosphere, absorb the sensations that the places gives you. It is your place and therefore it is perfect.

Try to have the same place in mind every time you do this practice. If you change your ideal place you have to go through the procedure again 3-9 times before you can continue to the second part, even if you have been doing the practice for a while.

Part 2: Meeting your Parents

Enjoy the atmosphere of your ideal place for a few minutes using all the inner senses. Now you are ready to mentally invite your parents to your ideal place.

You see your parents coming from afar, and as they enter your ideal place, they go and sit opposite you. You look at each other, but it is not necessary to say anything. You allow your eyes and your heart to unite and you allow any words or thoughts that exist to pass through the eyes and the heart so that an energy circuit is created. You observe what is happening. Speak or answer only if it is absolutely essential. Allow the words to become energy. Speak and listen "telepathically".

Think of your roots. Are they intertwined with those of your parents? Are your roots leading towards your parents' roots or are theirs coming towards yours? Are you more entangled with one of the two parents? Are their roots entangled more between them? Try to allow your roots to slip away effortlessly as you disentangle them.

When you feel you have done this, then allow your parents to leave. Your roots are no longer entangled and they are not found at the same place as theirs. LET YOUR PARENTS GO. Watch them leaving your ideal place.

You are alone again at your ideal place and are once again enjoying the atmosphere with all your senses. After a minute or two, become aware of your body in the room that you are currently in, and the position you are sitting in. Move your toes and your fingers and when you feel ready, open your eyes.

Additional notes:

1. This is a very important exercise which can change your life if done with full dedication. Sometimes we are so connected to our parents, in an invisible way that is not healthy at all. The aim of this practice is to 'cut' the 'unhealthy part' that connects children with their parents. However, it has to be done 3-6 times to be complete and effective.

2. If this practice is going to take place with a group, then they need to be informed of what is going to happen beforehand so as to give them the choice to take part or not take part in it, because they may feel they are not ready to face their parents or to let them leave. In such circumstances, the individuals who do not want to participate should leave the room.

3. Some people find it difficult to bring their parents to their own personal ideal place and others have problems letting them go. Both cases need to be dealt with so the invisible connections can be cut. This does not mean you will not see your parents again; on the contrary, you can now see them more frequently since the unhealthy parts of the relationship will have been removed.

4. The practice is the same even if your parents have passed away (you can still visualise them as being alive).

Life Practice
Perfecting Solitude

Numerous times during the practices on the first *Chakra*, various issues may come to the surface, such as: insecurities, fears, survival issues, experiences, situations with our parents or partner (who may sometimes replace our parents), pain in the pelvic area or the genital organs.

This is a sign that these practices may have stirred up certain situations. Observe them but do not do anything about them. Visit a doctor only if the symptoms or situations last for more than 3 weeks. The most likely reason for them, is that certain recollections that are no longer needed, are being dispensed with. Do not obstruct them. If we work regularly and correctly with the first *Chakra*, we will notice adjustments that we simply need to be aware of, and should let them do whatever they need to do, and then let them go.

It is a good idea to try and explore your relationship with your parents and your partner so you can see how much you depend on them and how independent you feel.

Learn to do things on your own that will allow you to enjoy your own company. Go for a meal on your own, go to the theatre, go for a walk on the seafront or in a park, cook a special meal and sit and enjoy it on your own, dress up nicely and then just sit at home and do some reading on your own.

Ask yourselves:
How comfortable do you feel on your own?
Do you enjoy your own company?
How much do you look after yourself?
Do you look after yourself, and keep your home clean and tidy only when there are people around?

Now is the time to do things to honour yourself!

A person who has a balanced first *Chakra*, can enjoy solitude and can receive the help or company of others as an extra pleasant surprise, and not as an absolute necessity.

Can you?

Weeks 22-24
Second Energy Center - Swadhisthana Chakra
(the seat of your personality)

SWADHISTHANA CHAKRA	Pelvis and Sacrum
	Body Part: **Intestines and Kidneys**
	Element: **Water**
	Hormonal Gland: **Adrenal**
	Converts *Prana* for:
	Pleasure/Food/Sex/Wellbeing
	It is blocked by: **Guilt**

The second energy centre is connected to the adrenal glands that sectrete the most 'popular' substance of our times – adrenaline. Adrenaline exists in our body so that it can increase our awareness in case of impending danger, so that we can defend ourselves or simply run away if needed (the three F's: Fright/fight/flight). In our modern day life we may not be in danger of being attacked by wild animals any more but adrenaline is secreted every time we are late for an appointment, when we feel our position is being threatened, when we watch a thriller on TV, when we have an important meeting, and more importantly when we panic about the future. Adrenaline is permanently in the blood of modern day human beings, so much so that they are now more dependent upon it than ever before. It is impossible for a human being to be calm anymore and it is impossible to stay away from thoughts. When we are not thinking, we believe that we are losing valuable time and if there is no tension or suspense in our life we think that life is dull. That is how strong our dependency on adrenaline has become. Of course, adrenaline makes humans wild and uncivilised. That is why we conceal the tension it brings on with the rules of social behaviour. What we show to others is not who we really are but what we call personality.

Under this permanent state of tension that has been created, personality has become very powerful. We do not know what we really want; we want what others want. We are not sure how to behave; so we behave like others do. We run around in a semi-hypnotised state searching for a new phone, car or flat; we want to try new tastes, buy new clothes, make new friends, until we discover that this is not what we really want. But even then, instead of looking inwards, we look around us to see what others want, so that we can want it too. The personality oppresses our real nature. And for this reason, we can never relax - or we are persistently inundated with feelings of guilt.

During the *asanas* (physical postures), our awareness should be at our kidneys, our adrenal glands (located above the kidneys) and our intestines. The *asanas* will gently 'massage' the kidneys and the glands in order to balance the amount of adrenaline which is now secreted automatically from them. In this way we can relax and we can see our real selves, and the personality can then become one with the Self. In addition to this, the intestines will be stretched and will be activated so that they can work correctly.

Ideas and memories related to our desires and pleasure (sex, food, wellbeing) are stored at the pelvis. The *asana* exercises also extend and increase the circulation of blood within the pelvic area so that they can 'digest' (and re-evaluate) possible ideas regarding sex, food, the need to have a good life and other various desires.

The visualisation of running water will help us tune with the element, and purify ourselves through this connection. In addition, water can help us tune with the quality of flexibility. Just as water takes the shape of the vessel it is in, in the same way we should be able to adjust to every situation without losing our Self. Although our natural state remains the same, our personality should be able to adjust according to the situation.

Physical Exercise

*These two asanas stretch the pelvis and the intestines and 'squeeze' the kidneys and therefore the adrenal gland, encouraging them to function properly. Choose **one of the two asanas** described below and hold the position for 1-3 minutes.*

1. *Supta Vajra Asana* - Extended Thunderbolt

Kneel down in *Vajra Asana (p.27)*. While breathing in, lean back and put your hands behind your body on the floor, and as you breathe out go even further back, bending first your left and then your right elbow on the floor behind you. When the two elbows are in the right place bring your head back so that it touches the floor.

Stay in this position for 1-3 minutes, trying not to lift your knees from the floor. Keep your awareness on your breath (abdominal breathing will make this practice more effective), on the stretching of the pelvis and the pressure on the kidneys.

After a while, visualise running water passing through the pelvis, rushing downwards and exiting from the tailbone.

2. *Sethu Asana* - The Bridge

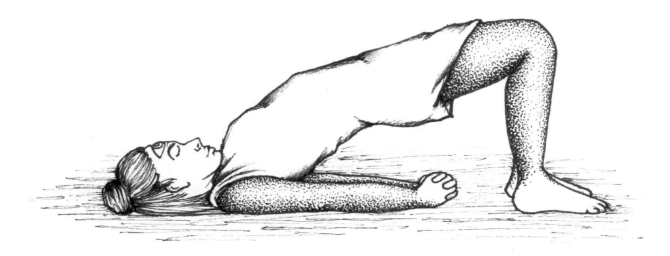

Lie on your back and bend your knees so that the heels are parallel on the floor, shoulder distance apart. Breathe in and lift your pelvis upward as much as you can until you feel that you are putting pressure on the kidneys.

Stay in this position for 1-3 minutes. Keep your awareness on your breathing (abdominal breathing will make this practice more effective), on the stretching of the pelvis and the pressure on the kidneys.

After a while, visualise water passing through your pelvis from above and exiting from the sides of the pelvis.

Meditative Breathing
Kaya Kriya 1 - Body-Breathing Action (Part 1)
(From the Gitananda Yoga tradition)

Lie flat on your back with your head facing the north, your legs and arms slightly apart and the palms of your hands looking upwards.

Start with some abdominal breathing.

After about 9 rounds, inhale and start rolling your feet inwards so that the big toes of your feet touch each other and are also touching the floor. With your out-breath roll the feet outwards so that the little toes touch the floor.

The movement should start from your thighs, allowing your whole leg to rotate. Do 9-27 rounds combining breath and movement. Then stay motionless for about 5 minutes and visualise a continual flow of water from the head to the feet.

This practice is excellent for cleansing and energising the pelvic area and the second *Chakra*. It mainly deals with the physical and psychological situations, for conditions that start from the body (accidents, bad physical habits, abuse or violent actions towards the body) that can affect us psychologically and mentally.

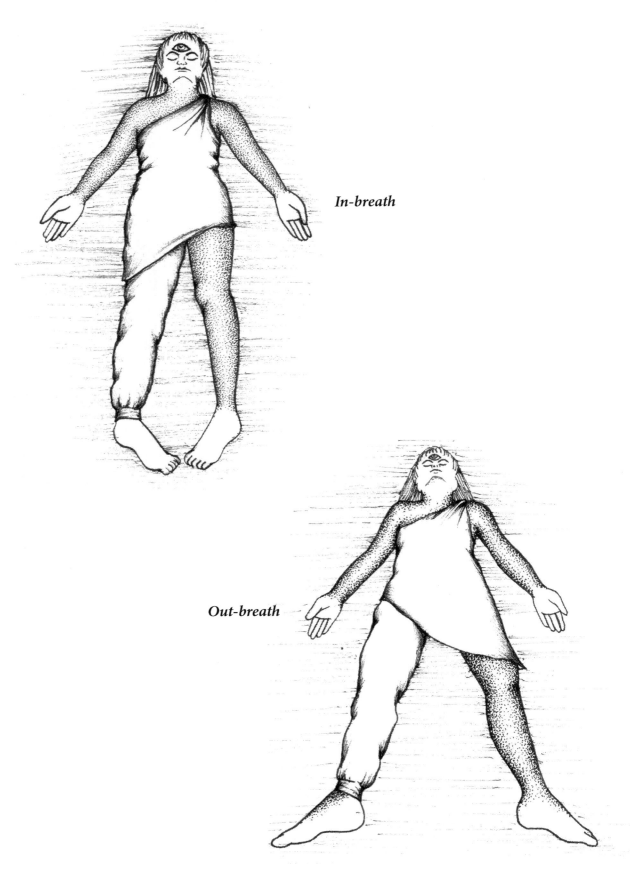

In-breath

Out-breath

Kaya Kriya

Mental Exercise
Active Detachment from Sexual Partners

Note: You need to have completed the "Ideal Place" practice (p.82) at least 3 times, as well as the detachment from your parents (p.83), before you attempt this practice.

Go to your ideal place passing through the "open market". After staying there alone for a while, enjoying the atmosphere, invite someone with whom you had a sexual connection in the past, or you are connected with now. Sit opposite each other and gaze at each other for a while. You do not need to talk to each other. Allow the unspoken words to become energy that pass through the eyes and the heart which are exchanged between you. If there is some conversation (or a monologue) do not try to obstruct it, just be aware of it.

Check your roots and if they are connected with the other person, let them become disentangled and then allow them to gradually slip away.

After 2-6 minutes allow the person to leave your ideal place. LET THIS PERSON GO. Watch them go and then remain on your own for 1-3 minutes.

When you are ready, realise where your physical body is, the room you are in, and your physical position, and start moving your fingers and toes to bring yourself back to the here and now.

This should be completed with all your previous lovers, until you are left with the one you are with now, and then you should complete the practice with him/her too.

Life Practice
Balanced Pleasure

Now is the time to sort out our relationship with the material world, food, and the way we perceive sex in order to be able to accept our own habits and qualities without having feelings of guilt, and to enjoy our lives as we would like, instead of simply emulating others. This will define our personality. A healthy personality adjusts to external factors, but at the same time expresses itself by being guided by the Self and not by the trends, social pressure and interests of other people or situations.

The material world and welfare:

One of the ethical codes of yoga is called *Aparigraha* which means that we should only possess what we need at a materialistic, mental and emotional level. If we follow this code we will cleanse the second *Chakra*. During this period when we are working on the second *Chakra*, I ask my students to bring something which is valuable to them, that they like, but they never use. They describe it and then leave it in the middle of the circle that we have created. This is a symbolic act that encourages us to finally be able to let go of what we do not really need starting at the materialistic level.

Food

This is not the time for fasting or for dieting. In this period we also explore our relationship with food. We observe what we eat without critique and without excuses. Every time you eat, give yourself a point based on the following list, according to the reason you are eating. After three weeks, add up the points and examine the real reasons you are eating. Just that.

1. I eat when I am hungry.
2. I eat before I am hungry so that I don't have the sense of hunger.
3. I eat because it is time to eat.
4. I eat because I like the taste of a particular food/dessert.
5. I eat to please someone else.
6. I eat for pleasure (at a restaurant, with friends etc).
7. I eat because I am alone.
8. I eat to keep my mind off my thoughts/feelings.
9. I eat because I don't know if I will have another opportunity to do so.
10. I eat because I feel weak if I don't eat.
11. I eat because… (*complete accordingly*)

Sex: How erotic are you?

Although in the previous century sexual activities often led to isolation and secrecy, nowadays if someone is not sexually active they may be looked down upon. Sexuality is not the same for all people neither in quality nor in quantity. Only if we project what we really are can we attract people who we will match with.

Sex is an technical way of relating to another person. Before you connect with someone sexually you should ask yourselves: *do I really want this invisible connection with the specific person?* Many people are eternally connected by marriage and family with completely unsuitable people, going against their own personal development.

Discover the real way you want to express yourself sexually. Don't be influenced by movies and what is happening around you. Fight any kind of guilt. Every person expresses his or her sexuality depending on his most active energy chakra. Each energy centre expresses itself in a different way, so if two partners are coordinated to the same energy centre when they are having sexual intercourse, then anything is acceptable as long as there is purity of intention and lack of guilt.

1. **First Chakra:** I have sex out of biological need, to keep my family together or to have a child.
2. **Second Chakra:** I have sex for pleasure.
3. **Third Chakra:** I have sex to conquer or be conquered, out of need to belong to someone, or for someone to belong to me.
4. **Fourth Chakra:** I connect with my partner to make someone that I love happy, and this makes me content.
5. **Fifth Chakra:** I become one with my opposite to share my completeness.
6. **Sixth Chakra:** I unite with my twin flame so that we become a unified force.
7. **Seventh Chakra:** I reunite with my twin flame, and I surrender this union to the higher cosmic good.

In Greek language there is a special word referring to the sexual connection: sinousia (συνουσία). Sin (connection/same) + ousia (essence) = the same essence.

Weeks 25-27
Third Energy Center: Manipura Chakra
(The Brightest Jewel)

MANIPURA CHAKRA

Solar Plexus (*Above the bellybutton*)
Body Part: **Stomach**
Element: **Fire**
Hormonal Gland: **Pancreas**
Converts Prana for: **Will and immediate action**
It is blocked by: **Inactivity**

The third energy centre is the centre of fire. This is where we 'digest' food, situations and emotions. It is not a coincidence that we often say things such as 'I really can't digest this idea' or 'I have butterflies in my stomach' or similar phrases relating to the stomach when we have specific problems or when something happens to us. Just like undigested food can create malfunctions/health issues and the production of toxins, in the same way undigested situations create psychosomatic conditions that may harm us. Therefore when we work with the solar plexus we try to increase the element of fire within us so we can burn the physical, emotional and mental residues that are created. We do this with postures that stimulate the stomach, the pancreas and the liver and with the visualisation of fire/sun/lit candles*.

Fire is the element of complete cleansing. If we wash something with water, the dirt will be removed but not destroyed. If we bury something in the ground, it will change form but it will not disappear - unless it is burnt.

Fire is also connected with direct action. There are no limitations with fire: it gives us light, it warms us, it cooks and heats food and liquids, it burns. We can manage fire to a certain extent, but we cannot change its energy. In the same way if we connect with this element we can encourage a more powerful and specific form of action.

* For the purposes of safety I have replaced the image of fire with the image of the sun or a lit candle. In this way the practice is toned down, and is therefore more appropriate for everyone in the group.

Physical Exercise
Dharmica Asana - The Devotion Pose

Kneel down in *Vajra asana (p.27)*. Breathe out and bend forward until your head is touching the floor without lifting your buttocks from your heels. Try to get your forehead as close to your knees as possible. Your hands are touching your feet. The spinal cord is slightly curved upwards; this will help stimulate the stomach. Stay in this position for 1-3 minutes.

Visualise a wonderful golden sun lighting the area of the solar plexus (stomach) and from there extend it to the whole of the nervous system, purifying it. When done, breathe in and sit up.

This posture stimulates the digestive system, releases tension from the spinal cord and increases the circulation of the blood in the head.

Meditative Breathing
Friction of the Spinal Cord

Lie on your back (*Shava Asana, p.32*) or sit in one of the meditative positions with a straight back. Do a quick journey of the 22 parts of the body. (*MarManasthanam Kriya, p.45*). When you are aware of your body, 'empty' it, until you feel it is hollow, with just the spinal cord inside. The body has its normal shape but inside there are no organs, muscles, bones; it is completely hollow with the exception of the spinal cord which separates the right side from the left.

Then start breathing through the nose making sure the inbreath is the same length as the outbreath. For example, 6 seconds for the inbreath, 6 seconds for the outbreath. When you inhale feel your awareness rising along the spinal cord, to the empty skull. When you exhale your awareness goes down from the head, along the spine to the tailbone. Continue this action a few times and then speed up the rhythm, always making sure that the inbreath and outbreath have the same duration. After about 20-30 rounds, continue with the rhythm of 4:4 for about 20-30 breaths, then 2:2 and 1:1 and finally complete it with one breath per second continuing the same visualisation up and down the spine for 20-30 breaths.

Then at this point, keep the motion going up and down the spine WITHOUT CO-ORDINATING YOUR COGNITIVE MOVEMENT WITH YOUR BREATH. The breath is now free and the awareness will still be moving up and down the spine. This "friction" of the breath and the visualisation creates heat which we allow to warm up our empty internal body.

When you feel you have completed this practice, imagine that your body is full again, revived and refreshed. Take a deep breath, move your fingers and open your eyes.

Please note: if you plan to follow the meditative breathing with the mental activity, first 'bring back' the body and continue immediately with the visualisation of the internal sun, and not with the polarity breath which is described on the following page.

Mental Exercise
Internal Sun

Lie on your back (*Shava Asana, p.32*) or in any comfortable meditative position with your spine straight. Do the polarity breath for 1-27 rounds. At a chosen point let your awareness take your breath from the legs to the third energy centre – just above the belly button, within your body, in front of your spinal cord.

Imagine that the source of your internal sun is located there. Look at your internal sun, golden and bright, and feel its warmth. Gradually the sun becomes bigger and warmer, until it covers the whole abdominal area, internally. Our solar plexus is located in this area; the largest nervous plexus. From this nerve plexus, the fire of the sun, golden yellow and superbly bright, will pass through the whole nervous system.

Watch your nervous system light up as if bursting into flames, with a purifying red-blue fire, all the way to the tips of your fingers and the top of your head. Stay like this for a few moments, and feel how warm and bright the nervous system is. Wherever there are impurities, they will burn, creating a sound as if they have been 'electrocuted', or similar to a crackling fire.

When you feel that the whole nervous system has been purified, allow your internal sun to shrink and to be confined again within the solar plexus, and then shrink it further to the size of the wick of a candle, at the third energy centre. Feel and see how clean, fresh, strong and healthy* your nervous system is; like a precious decorative ornament.

Take a deep breath, move your little finger and open your eyes.

It is essential that we 'end' the burning process within us, otherwise the fire element might become so strong that it makes us generally hyperactive. However, if we complete it and allow the body to recover we will experience purification and strength.

Life Practice
The burning of Experiences

Now is the time to 'digest' situations that have made our lives difficult. The essence of life is to eventually take the 'gift' from every experience and to discard the experience itself. When a child touches a socket and gets an electric shock, this will teach him not to play with electricity. But if the child cries each time that he sees a socket after this event, the outcome might be that he cannot use sockets or is scared to use them when he grows up; this shows that he did not 'digest' the experience. So learn to digest your experiences! Absorb whatever is needed and get rid of whatever is not necessary.

Remember that a great deal of what we are doing in yoga is to get rid of mental, emotional and physical toxins. Only then can we change the programming which is inhibiting our development. When we were working with the first *Chakra*, we allowed our roots to transfer whatever we didn't need into the earth, with the second *Chakra* we allowed water to wash the toxins away. With the third *Chakra*, we are burning our rubbish. This is actually the most effective method because fire is the most purifying of all the elements. The only thing that is left after a fire is ash. This is very good but also dangerous. If you ever practice the fire visualization, remember to see flowers growing from the ashes.

Remember to extinguish the fire after every visualisation. Never complete a visualisation or breathing practice without allowing the body to restore itself first – so you can see it revived without the fire.

If we can use it safely, fire will become a very effective tool in our life because it helps create a healthy digestive system. Observe it. The people with a strong digestive system are more decisive and can overcome their traumatic experiences faster. People who have problems with the digestive system or are constipated, hold on to the situation that occur to them like misers. Of course these two are interconnected and can go both ways.

In the period that we carry out these practices, we meet up with the group, we light a fire in a safe place, and we ceremoniously burn an object that symbolically represents something that we feel must end. It is a very nice ceremony which always feels like a kind of celebration and everybody leaves feeling purer. It is also a good opportunity to meet up with friends and to be able to offer them something useful: purification. We usually invite people from outside the group as well, and this tends to make the outcomes stronger. The more people, the stronger the experience. During the ceremony, some might briefly explain what they are going to burn when it is their turn, while others just silently pause for a minute before throwing their object into the fire. The power of the group can be so strong that there is not always a need for many words. The most significant thing is for everyone to have the same objective.

Weeks 28-30
Fourth Energy Center: Anahata
(The sound which has no origin)

ANAHATA CHAKRA	**Center of the chest** Body Part: **Heart** Element: **Air** Hormonal Gland: **Thymus** Converts Prana for: **The sense of oneness with everyone and everything, boundless love.** It is blocked by: **Emotional pain**

From the fourth chakra onwards, we start working on developing the more 'human' aspect of our nature, so there is not so much to be done physically. Although we usually say the solar plexus is the centre of the body, when a person evolves, the centre is transferred to the heart. Actions do not originate from the centre of the will anymore, but from the centre of love. This is a big step. Someone who wants to act through the heart must be sure that he or she has purified his animal nature first, which is represented by the first 3 *Chakras*. If he does not do this, he will hurt and be hurt repeatedly. **Only a 'complete' person can live and give love without expectations.** Animals cannot do this because they do not have the correct mechanism to do so. It might appear that our dog loves us unconditionally, but what is happening is actually more one-dimensional: it simply has a built-in program which tells it to care for the person from whom it obtains shelter, food, or even simple attention.

Our parents do not love us selflessly either. They may do so eventually, but first they have to ensure their child's need for survival (*first Chakra*), the need to belong and be accepted in society (second *Chakra*) and the need to dominate (third *Chakra*) and above all they have to get rid of the illusion of separation. Only then can they love their children unconditionally, without expectations.

The Illusion of Separateness

There is a very strong sign that the heart *Chakra* is open: we can no longer separate space, time or people. We have connected with the vibration of the universe (the sound which has no origin) and we accept everything without criticism or judgement. In this way we cannot hurt or be hurt.

Note: this does not mean that we should suddenly accommodate everything and everyone in our lives. We simply select and separate, in a painless way, who or what we will keep close to us.

"I love everyone, but I like very few..."
Yogamaharishi Dr Swami Gitananda

The thymus gland, along with the pituitary and pineal gland which are found in the brain, secrete a 'cocktail of hormones' which activate the experience of the inseparable. All of these three glands underperform in the average human being. This is why when I start describing the illusion of separateness, the response is a series of logical questions attempting to grasp what I am saying. However, when we begin working and our heart starts opening, then there is no longer a need for questions, and words lose their meaning - we simply feel.

With the physical practice for the fourth *Chakra*, we try to stimulate the thymus gland in a way that it can connect with the glands in the brain during the mental and breathing practices, so that we can experience the inseparable. This is not something permanent. The heart might soon become passive again, but at least we have experienced our ideal target for a while.

"Yoga helps us experience the fact that we cannot cut a flower without disturbing the stars."
Yogamaharishi Dr Swami Gitananda

Physical Exercise
Ardha Matsyendra Asana - Yogi Mastyendra's twist

Start in a sitting position, and then cross your right knee over the left and bend the left leg back. Use your left knee and the left hand to twist as much as you can towards the right. The buttocks should remain on the floor. Hold this position for 1-2 minutes and then change sides.

Feel a gentle breeze passing through the area of the heart.

The twisting action stimulates the thymus gland which is not fully functional in adults. In addition, it stimulates the nerves and improves the circulation of blood in the area of the spinal cord.

Meditative Breathing
Kaya Kriya 2 - Body Action (Part 2)

Lie down in *Shava Asana* (p. 32) with your head facing North, the legs are slightly open and the arms and hands are close to the body.

Start with some slow breaths using the middle part of the lungs. After about 9 breaths start breathing in from the chest, and allow the arms and hands to slowly turn outwards with the inbreath and inwards with the outbreath. The movement must start from the shoulders. Do 9-27 rounds coordinating this movement with the breath. Stay still for at least 3 minutes and then move on to the mental exercise.

This practice is excellent for cleaning and energising the area of the heart and the fourth energy centre. It frees mostly psychosomatic conditions; in other words, conditions that originate from our emotions and thoughts, and ultimately affect our physical body.

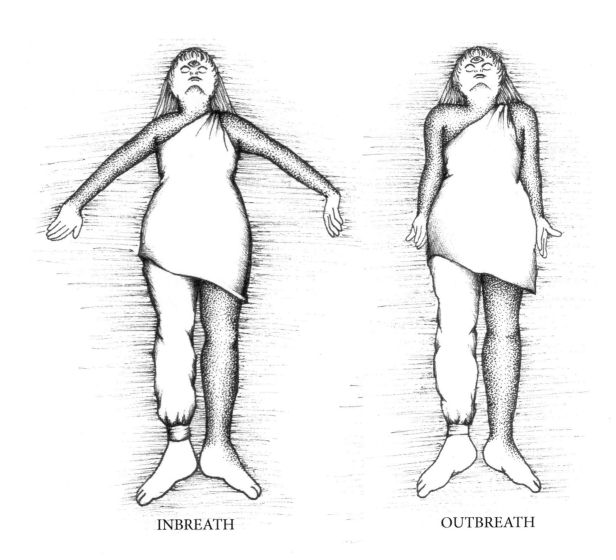

INBREATH   OUTBREATH

Mental Exercise
Flower on the Heart

Lie on your back (*Shava Asana, p.32*) or sit in any meditative position with a straight back. If you have not done the previous exercise, then it is better to do a quick journey of the 22 body parts first. (*Marmanasthanam Kriya, p.45*).

Do 9 rounds of polarity breath. At a chosen moment, transfer your breath and awareness from your feet to the centre of your chest. Start to imagine there is a tiny point, like a seed, there, on your chest. Visualise and feel that this seed is slowly coming to life and is becoming a beautiful flower. Any type of flower will do. The stem of the flower runs through your spinal cord to the ground and grows roots in the earth. The flower blooms and sits at the centre of your chest. You can almost smell the blossomed flower. Watch it grow as much as that type of flower can grow. Observe its colour. Feel the petals moving gently with the movement of your breath as you breathe in and out.

After a few moments and after you have experienced the flower with all your senses, imagine there is a breeze and that the petals are moving with the breeze. Then the breeze turns to rain and your flower welcomes this with gratitude. The rain becomes stronger but the drops slide over the petals, which remain dry and unaffected. The rain then turns to snow which again falls on the flower, which again remains unaffected by it. The ends of the petal turn white from the snow but don't freeze. Finally, the sun comes out, which melts the snow and gradually warms our flower. The warmth becomes very strong and the rays of the sun are very strong but again your flower opens and absorbs the heat and the light without any damage being caused. Allow your flower to absorb this light and warmth.

When you have completed this exercise, slowly become aware of your body in the room, start moving your hands and feet and open your eyes.

Mental Exercise 2
Active Detachment from your loved ones

This practice should only be attempted after the previous mental activity has been done at least 3 times, and ONLY if we have also completed the other 3 active detachment practices:
1. Ideal Place (alone)
2. Active detachment from our parents
3. Active detachment from romantic partners

Go to your ideal place, passing through the 'market'. After spending some time there alone, enjoying the atmosphere, invite the person that you love the most. Sit opposite each other and look at each other for a while. There is no need to talk. Allow your love to surround this person and to create a bright flow of energy between you.

Check to see if your roots are entangled and, if so, untangle them until they slip away gently.

After a few moments get ready to allow this person to leave. Prepare yourself mentally and ALLOW THIS PERSON TO LEAVE. Watch this person leave your ideal place without allowing him/her to look back, and bid this person to go wherever his higher nature wants to as he/she is leaving.

Stay on your own for 1-3 minutes enjoying the atmosphere of your ideal place. Then become aware of where you physical body is, the room that you are in, the posture that you are in, move your little finger and transfer your mind back to the here and now.

This practice can be carried out with all the people you love. This will give you the chance to refine your love for everyone, allowing full freedom from each other. This does not mean that you will lose this person; on the contrary, you will have a sense of freedom that strengthens the relationship further.

"The free soul is rare, but you know it when you see it - basically because you feel good, very good, when you are near or with them"
Charles Bukowski (Poet/Author)

Life Practice
Hugs

This is the time to learn to hug each other. It is not a matter of how many times we hug each other, but *how* we hug each other. We hug for 3 reasons:
1. To give energy
2. To take energy
3. To exchange energy

When a hug occurs for the exchange and not to take or give, everyone wins!

'Love is profound interest'
Yogamaharishi Dr Swami Gitananda

Once our heart is open, we feel this endless freedom which then becomes a life habit. A free spirit neither asks nor pressurises another to give. It does not demand, but neither does it show disinterest, and this is what makes others want to be near this free spirit. If we can show *interest* in someone deeply without becoming a nuisance, then we have managed to give the freedom that someone needs in order to bloom and develop.

We can work on all the above, practicing with our hugs. Let us hug those that we truly love, without being tenacious. Do not ask for anything when you are hugging. Just visualise a circle or the infinity shape flowing between the heart that connects us and concentrate only on this. The more we hug, the more opportunity we have to train ourselves to love as 'profound interest' and not as a need (first *Chakra*) or for passion (second *Chakra*) or for power (third *Chakra*).

"Neither love nor truth is for the weak.
Both are the inheritance of the dynamic and the strong."
Yogamaharishi Dr Swami Gitananda
(Yoga Step By Step course - lesson 15, page 57)

Weeks 31-33
Fifth Energy Center: Vishuddhi Chakra (Crystal Purity)

VISHUDDHI CHAKRA	**Throat** Body Part: **Base of the neck** Element: **Ether** Hormonal Gland: Thyroid Converts Prana for: **The expression of our true Self** It is blocked by: **Lies**

He who truly possesses correct human qualities and is not influenced by his animal nature any more, is pure at all levels. **Purity at all levels means that what is thought, what is shown and what is said are all in agreement** and this is an indication that the personality is serving the true Self. In this way, the natural connection which exists between the 'seat' of the personality (second *Chakra*) and the real nature (fifth *Chakra*) is healthy and both reinforce each other.

In order for someone to find his true, pure nature, he first needs to have safety and confidence (first *Chakra*), to have become independent of the masses (second *Chakra*) and to have freed himself from the pull of ambition (third *Chakra*). Only then can this person express the quality of the soul with crystalline purity.

For as long as the real Self is smothered by the personality however, there will be a permanent and very useful blockage at the neck, which will inhibit the immature person from developing. Some hasty practices unnaturally forcing the *kundalini* energy to the brain, without the person being ready to handle this energy ethically, will lead to delusions, ridiculous conduct, or at its best, eccentric actions that have absolutely no place in the behaviour of a truly developed mind.

Physical Exercise
Paripurna shasha asana - Extended Rabbit Pose

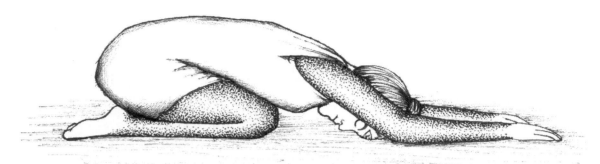

Shashanga Asana

Kneel down and sit on your heels (*Vajra Asana* p.27). While breathing out, bend your head forward till it touches the floor (*Shashanga Asan*a) and then roll the head forward while breathing in, lifting the buttocks up from the heels while at the same time making sure that the chin is pressing the base of the neck.

Paripurna Shasha Asana

Stay in this position for 30 seconds at first (after a few sessions, when you feel the nape is strong enough, keep this position from one to three minutes). Visualise a never ending clear blue sky.
If you have a problem with your nape, try using your elbows to hold and protect your neck and to keep the pose better. The chin should always press the base of the neck to stimulate the thyroid gland.*

Then, while breathing out sit back on your heels with your head on the floor (*Shashanga Asana*) and after staying in this position for a while, get back to the original kneeling position (*Vajra Asana, p.27*). This practice brings awareness, en-

110

ergy and increases the circulation in the neck and head, while safely stimulating the thyroid gland.

Stimulation of the gland means encouraging the gland to function more effectively. This means that if it is overworking it will calm down and if it is passive it will be activated.

Meditative Breathing
Ujai pranayama- Psychic Breath
(From the Satyananda Yoga Tradition)

Sit in a meditative pose, ensuring that the spinal cord is straight (lie down only if it is necessary). Do some rhythmic breathing from the nose (in 6, out 6). Now bring your awareness to the throat and visualise that you are breathing from the larynx and not through the nose. A sound will be made that sounds like gentle snoring or like a baby sleeping.

This is the psychic breath. Concentrate on the sound that remains in your throat from this breathing. This sound must not be loud and should only be heard if someone comes up really close to you.

Continue this breathing for 6-9 minutes.

Next, continue psychic breathing, concentrating on the sound, without trying to control the rhythm too much, for as long as you want. Experience this movement of ether that is formed through the breathing. Realise that ether is a more refined form of air charged by the breath.

This psychic breath helps the energetic purification of the fifth *Chakra* but also of the nervous system, it enhances concentration and focuses on the more refined level of the mind.

Mental Exercise
The Self

This practice should only be attempted if we have also completed the other 4 detachment practices:
1. Ideal Place (alone)
2. Energetic detachment from our parents
3. Energetic detachment from romantic partners
4. Energetic detachment from our loved ones

If the above detachments are not insalled, this practice will have a different result however, because what will be created in the visualisation described below will come from the 'Ego' and will not have any therapeutic value.

Go to your ideal place, passing through the market. After staying alone there for a while, you see a figure approaching you and you close your eyes.

You feel this person coming near and sitting opposite you. Stay there with closed eyes for a while and feel this person who is sitting opposite you. Do you feel secure? Do you feel safe? Does this person feel amicable? Do you feel that you can trust this person even though you do not know who they are? Think about it and answer without judging or criticising.

When you are clear about how you feel, open your eyes. The person sitting opposite you is YOU; a more superior form of you however, one who is free from trauma, complexes and prejudices. Sit and look at each other for a while. There is no need to speak. Gradually create a bright energetic flow between you.

When you feel that this current is at its strongest, both of you will take a step forward so that one goes inside the other and you become one. Now you have your superior form within you.

Stay alone, complete, for 1-3 minutes enjoying the atmosphere of your ideal place.

Then, realise where your physical form is, the room that you are in, the pose that you are in, move your little finger and slowly bring your mind back to the here and now.

Mental Exercise 2
Absolute Self-Expression
(From "Pleasure Lab" - www.yorgosk.com/pleasurelab)

As we also run a theatre group (www.theatrotranscendental.weebly.com) we can focus on physical and aural expression. We all gather in an open space and we let our bodies move freely for at least an hour. We need at least half an hour to co-ordinate what we really want regarding our body movement. Once this is done, we start making sounds, primitive ones sometimes, that express what we feel and want to let go of at that point. We continue with the movement and sound for another hour and then we create a one-minute piece of physical, self-expression that expresses what we are at that given moment, freed from our subconscious burden. We then present our piece to the group.

Life Practice
The Creation of Beauty and the Three-fold Communication

Now is the time to allow our true nature to express and create. There isn't a more effective way of expression than that which occurs through art. Art can bring our true self to the surface in a symbolic way. At first maybe only our 'junk' comes out. However, if we work with ethos and regularity, the junk will disappear and then our real nature will flourish, inspiring others to do the same.

True art is not that which is preferred by the majority of people, nor that which is approved of by the critics. True art is that which is free from subconscious non-sense and inspires both artists and their audience to find their higher nature. This is what Aeschylus, Beethoven, Chekov, Michelangelo, Kazantzakis and so many other artists did. So let us therefore find a way to express ourselves through art.

Let us create something beautiful, that has not been done before, with the aim of communicating with our higher selves and that of our fellow humans. It might be a poem, a painting, a literary piece, choreography and so much more. It can even be a beautiful garden, a lovely bouquet, a wonderful decoration or anything else which comes from your soul.

Create and express yourselves!

"Every day, create a beauty that does not yet exist."
Buddha

The creation of something beautiful will encourage us to experience our true Self, and will activate self value. Self value will lead us to work towards the **three-fold communication of solitude, companionship and social life**. Certainly, depending on our experiences and tendencies, we will have preferences regarding communication. For a well-balanced person, however, no type of communication is a problem. In our relationships we have to experience all types of communication, so that we can take and give whatever life offers so we can evolve.

A complete person seeks and feels comfortable spending lots of time on his own (solitude). The complete person has created close, peaceful relationships which help him develop and contribute (companionship). The complete person co-exists comfortably with the world (social) without feeling awkward with strangers or panicking with criticism.

In this period we focus on the three-fold communication and encourage all three parts, with self value as a tool.

Weeks 34-36
Sixth Energy Center - Ajna Chakra
(Intuitive Knoweldge)

AJNA CHAKRA	**Point between the eyebrows** Body Part: **Center of the brain** Element: **Mind** Hormonal Gland: **Pituitary** Converts Prana for: **The knowledge which does not come from what we learn, but what we intrinsically know** It is blocked by: **The illusion which is randomly created from the interference of the ego with inherent knowledge.**

During this period, we work on directing energy to the brain so that we can 'awaken' the most important gland of our system; the pituitary gland, and in this way we can begin the process of our awakening. However, this can only occur after the acquisition of a disciplined practice which is used in conjunction with good character. If not, we will just enjoy clearer thoughts and better concentration of the mind, but nothing more.

The pituitary and the pineal gland are two interconnected glands which in addition to governing the whole of the hormonal system and having many other important physical and psychological functions, are also responsible for our awakening. In most cases, these glands are underactive as they function only for our survival. If they are stimulated further, the mind can slowly emerge from its lethargic state. This does not happen to everyone however, purely because they do not have the energy and the ethos to use a powerful, awakened mind. Typically, we only use a small fraction of the qualities of the brain because if it is fully awakened, we may destroy ourselves and all those who are around us. It is for this reason that for thousands of years now the practices which can awaken the mind have remained a secret. We have deactivated telepathy, intuition, intuitive knowledge and so much more, purely because due to the illusion of separateness (See the thymus gland and *Anahat Chakra*), we have managed to lose our ethos and think only of ourselves. In this era, only the people who can work collectively and not individually can be awakened. The rest, however many practices they may do, will simply feel some bursts of power, a sense of wellbeing and serenity, but won't go any further.

Often, energy does not rise up to the brain because of our *Samskara* (deeply rooted knowledge resulting from experiences, trauma, egoistical tendencies, prejudices and bias). Every time we 'cleanse' ourselves of some of our *Samskara* however, even a little, it is like opening a single 'fibre' from the big 'energy cable' which connects our vital energy and the energy of the Source (God). This psychic energy cable is found alongside the spinal cord and passes into the brain and beyond. When our vital energy is connected with the Source, it produces light. This internal light awakens and stimulates the brain and all its higher qualities.

The biggest disagreement in spiritual circles is which of the aforementioned should come first - The awakening itself or the activation of the pituitary gland?

The Jnana Yogis are involved with the philosophy and psychology of the human brain, and they have come to believe that through their research and life practice they are led to enlightenment and in this way, the pituitary gland is activated. The Kriya Yogis, however, concentrate more on practices which lead to the awakening of their vital energy and its guidance towards the brain in such a way that the pituitary gland is activated and this will bring enlightenment.

The truth is that a combination of both can produce results without side effects, illusions and time consuming complications. The system which combines both paths is the system of *Raja Yoga* (the Royal Path).

The system of *Raja Yoga* was recorded by Patanjali, many thousands of years earlier. It comprises eight steps with the last one being the attainment of complete absorption by the Source (*Samadhi*).

The eight steps of awakening are:

1. *Yama* – Social Code (for the prevention of *Karma*)
2. *Niyama* – Personal Code (for burning *Karma*)
3. *Asana* – Steady, Comfortable Posture
4. *Pranayama* – Generation and Control of *Prana*
5. *Pratyahara* – Sensory Withdrawal
6. *Dharana* – 'One-pointness'
7. *Dhyana* – Meditation
8. *Samadhi* – Absorption by the Source

The eight steps towards enlightenment and absorption start with an ethical code that encourages the elimination of the Illusion of separateness. it is worth noting that one of the personal codes (*Niyama*) is to be able to feel that something higher exists; the Source from which we come and that we are attached to. We continue with the preparation of the body so that it can learn to stay completely still. The ability to be motionless is a very important part of our development. The mind cannot relax if the body is continuously moving. A person who has not worked with ethos cannot remain still. Confidence, guilt and active karmic energetic fibres can upset the body and make it unstable and stiff. At the same time that we are working on ethos we can also work on staying still so we can strengthen the spinal cord and the joints through various postures (*Asanas*). In that way we can achieve the final asana which will be the meditative pose. Our stillness will teach us to feel and consequently guide our vitality (*Prana*). The directing of vitality (*Pranayama*) occurs with exercises that use mind and breath simultaneously, since vitality moves through both of these. When we learn to direct our prana with our breath, then our aura becomes stronger and then we can direct the prana with the mind only. This will bring us to the fifth step which is the awakening of our senses and finally detachment from the senses and from life, so that we can understand that we are not what we perceive from our senses, what we think, or what is happening to us (*Pratyahara*). Only then can we concentrate on one point (*Dharana*) for a long period of time until the brain withdraws to higher levels of meditation. If this can last for enough time, and if our Karma allows it, then perhaps we can be absorbed by the Source (*Dhyana*). The absorption can be complete and then we are enlightened (*Samadhi*).

All the above information is useful for the aspiring student that wants to awaken the brain, but it may remain as mere knowledge to feed the ego, if it is not used in practice.

The main aim of this book is to give to the student a safe path full of actions which stretches up until the sixth step of *Raja Yoga* (*Dharana* – 'one-pointness'). Beyond that, meditation will be achievable if the student chooses it.

Physical Exercise
Parvat Asana - The Mountain Pose
& *Yoga Mudra* (From the Gitananda Yoga tradition)
& *Shabhani Mudra* (From the Satyananda Yoga tradition)

The physical postures that we usually do for the sixth *Chakra* are inverted postures and especially the ones that involve balance of the head. However, because the inverted postures need a lot of care and have a lot of side effects for those who do not have a pure system, we recommend an exercise which, if carried out with full concentration, will have very effective results.

Sit in the lotus position (*Padma Asana*) or in any other cross-legged pose that you feel comfortable in. Breathe in while raising your arms above your head with the palms of your hands connected (*Anjali Mudra*). This is *Parvat Asana* (mountain pose). Lift the pupils of your eyes as if you want to see the space between your eyebrows (*Shabhani Mudra*). The eyes could be open or closed. Keep your eyes like this for as long as you can without lifting your head. Relax your eyes as often as you have to. The unified hands above your head create an intense energy circuit at the head. Feel it. The position of the eyes immediately stimulates the nervous

118

system between the eyebrows and creates an energy 'antenna'. This antenna, when activated, receives messages from the 'universal library'. Stay in this position for 1 minute and then, at a chosen breath, bring your hands down, hold your left wrist with your right hand and bend forward until your head is released on the floor (if possible). Even if your head cannot reach the floor, allow the trunk of your body to fall forward as much as you can. This is the *Yoga Mudra*.

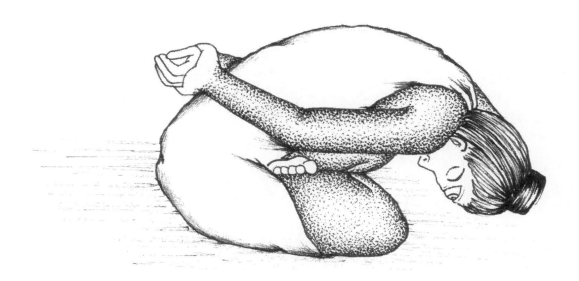

Yoga Mudra

Stay like this for 1-3 minutes. Then, breathing in, return to Parvat Asana and concentrate on Shahani Mudra mentally, repeating "om, om, om", feeling the vibration of the sound in the area of the Ajna Chakra (space between the eyebrows). Hold this for 1-2 minutes and relax.

Meditative Breathing

Prana Kriya
(From the Gitananda Yoga tradition)

Sit in a meditative posture with a straight spine. Make sure you are facing the north. Do some polarity breaths. At a chosen moment, bring your awareness from the pelvis to the centre of the brain (thalamus).

Continue breathing and transfer your awareness along a straight line to the point between the eyebrows and guide your breath in the following way:

Breathe in: Your awareness starts from the centre of the brain (thalamus), passing through the area between the eyebrows and emerging along a straight line out of the head, towards the horizon.

Breathe out: Your awareness comes from the horizon, enters the head through the space between the eyebrows, and when the lungs are empty, ends up at the centre of the brain (thalamus).

Repeat this for 1-27 rounds.

Finally, continue the visualisation without the breath for 3-9 minutes.

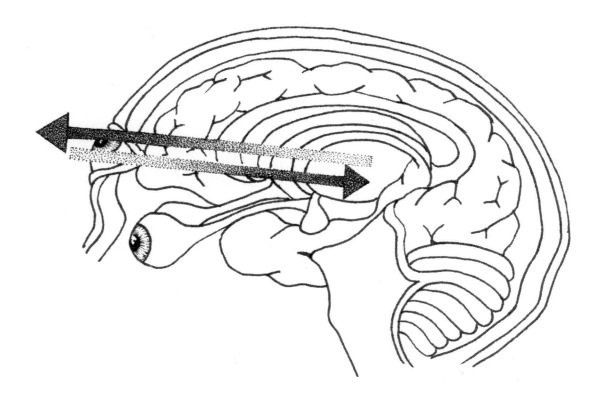

Mental Exercise
Cyclops' Eye (Part 1)

Concentrate on the pineal gland at the back of the head. Visualise it as a closed cone with the tip pointing towards the eyebrow. The cone slowly grows and opens.

The cone expands and moves forward within the area between the eyebrows and then transforms into a large eye like that of a Cyclops*, at the forehead.

The eye does not blink – feel it. It also feels all the senses, try it. 'See' with this eye. 'Hear', 'feel', 'smell' and 'taste' with this eye. Discover which of your internal senses is the strongest for you. Can you easily see visions? What is easier for you? To 'feel' situations, to 'smell' things that do not exist in the physical world? To 'hear' symbolic sounds that others cannot hear? To feel vibrations and tastes on your tongue when there is nothing there? These are your internal senses. Feel your third eye, and experiment with them.

When you feel you are done, CLOSE YOUR EYE, TRANSFORM IT BACK INTO A CLOSED CONE AND BRING IT BACK TO THE PINEAL GLAND. **Do not leave this eye open! Otherwise you will not be able to coordinate yourself in the world of logic.**

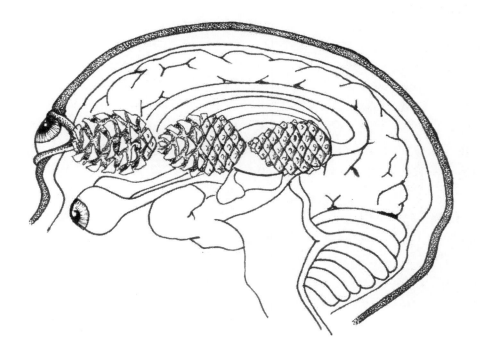

if you look at the top of a pinecone from above, you will see that it looks like the pupil of the eye. At first, this is how it looks in the space between the eyebrows, before it is transformed into an eye.

121

Cyclops' Eye (Part 2)

After you have completed the previous exercise enough times so that the third eye is activated, you are ready to ask a question. The answer will not come in any logical form, but in a symbolic way, through your most powerful internal sense. The knowledge you acquire can only be interpreted by you. You must never share these internal feelings with anyone. The world that we live in is based on external feelings and logic. **The experiences of the third eye cannot be applied to the external world.** Those who try to do this are just considered crazy. We should use the inner senses of the third eye to obtain symbolic information, that we can 'interpret' for the external world. The initial form of this information must be purely personal.

Life Practice
Intuition and Logic

The time has come for us to acknowledge whatever we are attempting to do in the spiritual world. There are two trains of thought to avoid: that of those who won't lose the opportunity to point out to those around them that they are involved in the spiritual world, and that of those who hide their efforts out of shame. Both bring the same obstacles to our spiritual development. We have to be able to express our attempts, but at the same time we have to accept we are on the path and not at the destination.

For as long as a person has a physical body, he is only on the path. It is an illusion to believe that we have reached somewhere if we still have physical limitations. Humility is necessary to weaken 'the ego' and to establish knowledge. Otherwise we will be filled with illusions that not even God can eliminate. The person who is truly enlightened is humble, because he knows that nothing matters anyway.

On the other hand, in the period we are living in, everything is challenged by science. Nothing can be considered true, unless it has been proven scientifically; Science is the new religion and it has exactly the same results religion has: it weakens intuition, it weakens the conscience, and demands full dependency on something *outside* of us. This is what we must fight, and we must dare to seek our own knowledge away from any information that may be trying to impose itself on us. Let us bravely declare that we will consult our own intuition, before resolving to any scientific or religious theory. Begin with what you are reading right now; rather than simply accepting the information, filter it through your intuition. *Feel* the practices, and through them create the core of your own internal experiences.

"Before enlightenment, you cut wood and carry water. After enlightenment, you cut wood and carry water."

(Zen saying)

Epilogue
Once we have organised the mind...

The time has come to start thinking about meditation. Meditation is the empty-ing of the mind and the concentration on this emptiness. Meditation can also be surrendering to something higher. Whatever that means to each of us, we need to cleanse and organise the 'system' (body, mind, feelings) before attempting medi-tation. If we neglect this step, it would be like mopping the floor without having swept up first. The dirt will simply spread evenly everywhere and we will think we are clean when we are not. This does not mean we have to wait until we are perfectly pure to begin meditating. But we must reach a certain satisfactory level of organisation. Organisation means self-knowledge.

There are two prerequisites for us to work with our self-knowledge, if we are to avoid the help of a psychoanalyst.

1. To be able to see life as a **workshop for the soul** and not as a struggle for the survival of our dignity.

2. To be able to see our imperfections as an opportunity to become stronger and not as something that we need to eliminate or ignore. **We must DIS-TILL the imperfections, not eradicate them.** Trying to fight our imperfec-tions head on, will turn them into monsters.

"Life is a cosmic dream. When you awaken, it no longer exists..."

(The Upanishads)

Kriya Yoga
The Yoga of Action

The system of *Kriya Yoga* is the system of action for purification. Every yoga tradition means something different when referring to *Kriya Yoga*. In essence though, all the traditions agree that *Kriya Yoga* is the *action* in the workshop which we call life. We can break *Kriya Yoga* down into three categories:

1. Specific mental and respiratory practices which are done in a specific order and which open centres of the brain and channel energy (not mentioned in this book). Before starting these practices it would be a good idea to cover all the physical exercises which are mentioned in this book from weeks 1 – 36, one after the other in the order mentioned. This will take about one and a half hours (with breaks between each one).

2. The action of life with the last 3 *Niyamas* (personal codes) as Pantanjali mentions them. This technique is the same as the spiritual practices that Christianity preaches. These are *Tapas* (discipline), *Swadhiyaya* (self-enquiry and pursuit of knowledge), *Ishwara Pranidhana* (surrender to the higher).

3. Complete devotion to the reactivation of our conscience and the perfection of ethos. This can occur with intensive work of the *Yamas* (social code) and *Niyamas* (personal code).

In order to perfect ethos through the Yama/Niyama code, we must undertake the following steps:
First step: Realisation (*"analysis brings solutions"*)
Second step: Action (*"When an action is not desirable, then we concentrate on its opposite"* – Pantanjali)
Third Step: Meditation (meditation 'burns' the layers that hide the truth).

Meditation
Absolute Absorption

Once we have cleansed the system (body, mind, emotions), then it is the time to approach the higher mind and the soul. This happens through meditation. After the yoga of action, comes the yoga of no action; When these two are combined, then the power of meditations appears. It is like a bird that flaps its wings very hard to reach a certain height, but once there it can let the current of the air take over. If the bird continues to flap its wings when it is in flight, then it will lose its way.

Now is the time to surrender.
What should we surrender to?

This is the individual seeker's choice.

"Divine existence of mine,
That which existed and will always exist
Take me into your service
I surrender my earthly being
I surrender my wishes, my fears, my prejudices, my persona
Enlighten me
So that I can use my abilities to the fullest
To serve humankind
Amen."

BIBLIOGRAPHY

Yoga Step By Step by Yogamaharishi Dr Swami Gitananda

Yoga Samyama by Yogamaharishi Dr Swami Gitananda

Frankly Speaking by Dr. Swami Gitananda Giri

A Yogic Approach to Stress by Dr. Ananda Balayogi Bhavanani

Yoga: 1 to 10 by Dr. Ananda Balayogi Bhavanani

Pranayama in the Tradition of Rishiculture Ashtanga Yoga by Dr. Swami Gitananda Giri, Yogacharini Meenakshi Devi Bhavanani and Dr. Ananda Balayogi Bhavanani

Chakras: The Psychic Centres of Yoga and Tantra by Dr. Ananda Balayogi Bhavanani

Mudras (New Edition) by Dr. Swami Gitananda Giri

Hatha Yoga Practices of the Rishiculture Ashtanga Yoga Tradition by Dr. Ananda Balayogi Bhavanani

Understanding the Yoga Darshan (An exploration of the Yoga Sutra of Maharishi Patanjali) by Yogacharya Dr Ananda Balayogi Bhavanani

Bhavana: Essays on Yoga Psychology by Yogacharini Meenakshi Devi Bhavanani

The Yoga Drishthi of Yogamaharishi Dr. Swami Gitananda Giri Guru Maharaj Compiled by Yogacharya Dr. Alan Davis

Yoga Nidra by Swami Satyananda Saraswati

A Systematic Course in the Ancient Tantric Techniques of Yoga and Kriya by Swami Satyananda Saraswati

Four Chapters on Freedom: Commentary on Yoga Sutras of Patanjali by Swami

Satyananda Saraswati

Sure Ways to Self Realization by Swami Satyananda Saraswati

Meditations from the Tantras by Swami Satyananda Saraswati

Prana, Pranayama, Prana Vidya by Swami Niranjananda Saraswati

Sri Vijnana Bhairava Tantra: The Ascent by Swami Satyasangananda Saraswati (Yoga Publications Trust)

Asana Pranayama Mudra Bandha by Swami Satyananda Saraswati

The Ayurvedic cookbook by Amadea Morngstar with Urmila Desai

Creative Visualization by Shakti Gawain

The Divided Brain and the Search for Meaning by Iain McGilchrist.

Zen Flesh Zen Bones: A Collection of Zen and Pre-Zen Writing by Paul Reps & Nyogen Senzaki

Left in the Dark. The Biological Origins of the Fall From Grace by Tony Wright and Graham Gynn

Man's Search for Ultimate Meaning by Viktor E. Frankl

Dhanwantari: A Complete Guide to the Ayurvedic Life by Harish Johari

The Chakra Book: Energy and Healing Power of the Subtle by Osho International Foundation

A New Earth: Methods, Exercises, Formulas and Prayers (Complete Works, Vol. 13) by Omraam Mikhael Aivanhov

The Science of Yoga by I. K.Taimini

The Yoga Vasistha by swami krishnananda

The Serpent Power by Arthur Avalon

The Ten Principal Upanishads put into English by Shree Purohit Swami and W.B.Yeats

Chakra & Kundalini Workbook: Psycho-Spiritual Techniques for Health, Rejuvenation, Psychic Powers & Spiritual Realization by Jonn Mumford

Karma Manual: 9 Days to Change Your Life by Jonn Mumford

Pharmacy for the soul by Osho

Έλεγχος του νου με τη μεθοδο Σιλβα Silva Jose, Miele Philippe

Η Μυστική Ερμηνεία του Θείας Λειτουργίας του Αγ. Ιωάννου του Χριστοστόμου Πρωτοπρεσβ. Ιωαννης Σιτάρας.

Τα απόκρυφα ευαγγέλια και ο σχηματισμός της Κ.Δ. Θεόδωρου Ρηγινιώτη, Εκδ. Πύρρα

Η Καινή Διαθήκη Όπως Διαδόθηκε από τους Εσσαίους Εσσαϊκή Αδελφότητα

Το Φως της Ψυχής Α. Μπέιλη

Μπάκγαβαντ Γκίτα μετάφραση Θ. Παντουβά

Yogalife - Chakra Course
With Korina Kontaxaki (Yogacharini Anandhi)
(Senior teacher at International Centre of Yoga Education and Research - India)

How to establish a new mental programming for awareness and wellness

The Yogalife Chakra Course is part of the Wholistic Spiritual Training program, and is directed at yoga teachers and those who are interested in learning about the philosophy and psychology of yoga.

It incorporates an initiation to yogic life and thought, and includes 18 lessons, which cover:

- The basic psychological/philosophical theories of traditional yoga.
- Specific meditative breathing (*Pranayama*) and physical poses (*Asanas*) which are related to each theory.
- Mental practices (*Dharana*) which establish the theories as programming of the mind.
- Life practices. The main part of the seminar are the 'life practices' which encourage the participants to experience things and to write about these experiences.
- Lessons are offered once every three weeks; written assignments and physical/breathing practices are also included.
- Personal sessions with Korina Kontaxaki regarding the meaning of the *Yantra Karma/Dharma Yuga* techniques; discovering your own personal path through the mystic science of numerology.

A certificate is given on completion of the course.

The course is also offered online/ through distance learning.

If you would like to know more, or sign up for the course, please email: **yogalife@cytanet.com.cy**

Anna Cosma - Illustrator

We discovered Anna making sketches to order, expressing the subconscious of her customers in her imaginative and quirky designs. She then began designing T-shirts and Tattoos, and is now a fully qualified tattoo artist in Cyprus. You can follow her on Instagram (annac.art) and facebook (@annacosma.art).

Printed in Great Britain
by Amazon